Merchant Ships and Shipping

Merchant Ships and Shipping

R. MUNRO-SMITH

SOUTH BRUNSWICK
NEW YORK: A.S. BARNES AND COMPANY

MERCHANT SHIPS AND SHIPPING.©
R. Munro-Smith 1968. First American
edition published 1970 by A.S. Barnes
and Company, Inc., Cranbury, New
Jersey 08512

Library of Congress Catalogue Card Number: 79-99930

SBN: 498 07544 3

Printed in the United States of America

1907329

CONTENTS

ILLUSTRATIONS

EDITOR'S NOTE

This series of books is primarily intended to be of interest to those professionally concerned with the design, construction and operation of ships and other marine vehicles. Many remarkable changes are now taking place in the size, shape, speed and capability of conventional ships of all types, while hovercraft, hydrofoil ships and other unorthodox vessels are beginning to have a striking effect on the maritime scene. Technical staff and management increasingly need up-to-date design data and specialist information on a wide range of topics, and it is hoped that most books in the series will be of direct value to them, and to many students at universities and technical colleges.

In addition to specialist monographs and student textbooks, the series also includes books having a broad appeal to all those who want to know more about the fascinating variety of craft which can be seen in ports, on rivers, and at sea. This book is one of that group and its principal purpose is to give the non-technical staffs of shipbuilding and shipping organisations a working knowledge of many of the topics associated with their work. For this reason it is written in simple language, as free as possible from complex technicalities, and this should also help others who do not have a professional concern with ships to know more about the different types of ship, how they are built, and the various regulations designed to ensure their strength and safety in all circumstances. There are, of course, several books which cover similar topics and each one naturally reflects to some extent the author's personal experience and interest. The author of this book has had long experience in lecturing to a wide range of students about ship subjects, and his account of merchant ships and shipping today is both thorough and up-to-date.

PREFACE

Shipbuilding and shipping are old and traditional fields of human activity. Men and merchandise have been carried by water since the dawn of time. Today the prosperity of this country rests upon the trade that is carried by sea and consequently the operation of merchant ships is a very important industry.

The great progress made in the shipbuilding and shipping industries in recent decades has been possible by the skills of the technical staffs engaged in the design and construction of ships, employees of shipping concerns dealing with the involved details of running a fleet of vessels, underwriters who are concerned with the risks associated with the insurance of ships and their merchandise, and the officers and crew upon whose knowledge of navigation and marine engineering so much depends. Shipping is still the only major British industry that is, at the moment, the biggest of its kind in the world.

In the post-war years the shipbuilding industry has successively been under the aegis of the Admiralty, the Minister of Transport, the Board of Trade and now the Ministry of Technology. This latter transfer was made because it was considered illogical to separate marine engineering from other aspects of the engineering industry. The shipping industry is made up of something like 400 companies. The ramifications of trades and types of ships are numer-

ous. Some of the shipping fleets, particularly those of the oil
companies, are owned by very large organisations of which
shipping is not a major part. Some ships are owned by British
subsidiaries of foreign firms and some British-crewed ships are
registered in Bermuda. It is thus quite a complex structure.

The pressure of world economic conditions on British shipbuilding
and shipping is constantly increasing and has brought many
changes in recent years. Probably the most striking changes in
ships during the last two decades are in size and speed. The former
is amply demonstrated by deadweight in a change from 20,000
tons to 200,000 tons for recent oil tankers. The speed of dry cargo
ships has changed from the region of 12 knots to more than 20 knots.
The development of navigational equipment, the adoption of
greater protective measures for the safety of life at sea, the introduction of centralised and remote control leading to outright
automation of ships, together with the development in marine
engineering, have called for a concentrated form of individual
training and an expansion of knowledge for those associated with
ships and shipping.

In order to design, produce and maintain the most efficient ship
of tomorrow it is essential that shipbuilder, shipowner, ship-
broker, chartering broker, marine insurer, surveyor, marine
engine builder, and ship repairer understand something of each
other's business. It is only in this way that these varied interests
can find common ground from which the best will spring. British
shipbuilding and shipping in the future will demand the utmost
effort by all concerned to keep pace with and draw ahead of the
formidable contemporaries.

The purpose of this book is to enable the non-technical staffs
associated with shipping operations to have a working knowledge
of the subjects associated with their profession and also make it
possible for the layman to take an intelligent interest in such
matters. The various chapters are written in simple language and
free from complex technicalities. Reference is made to the work
of the Inter-Governmental Maritime Consultative Organisation
(I.M.C.O.) and the statutory regulations arising from International
Conventions.

R. Munro-Smith

I · MERCHANT SHIP TYPES

Ships are designed, built and operated to fulfil requirements and limitations laid down by the owner. Trade route, port facilities, type and quantity of cargo, speed and accommodation for passengers are the primary factors which control ship design. There is a great variety of types of floating vessels, ranging from the large transatlantic liner to the non-propelled barge. The many varieties of cargoes transported by sea and the economic pressure exerted on operators by competition have brought about particular types of ships designed for specific purposes. No ship type today has reached finality in design.

From the point of view of construction, the type of ship is largely decided by the extent and arrangement of erections above the freeboard deck. Erections can affect the strength of the ship as a whole and consequently the scantlings of the main hull must be modified in relation to the extent and nature of the erections. Such erections must extend from side to side of the ship and may be short, long or complete. Short erections do not exceed 15 per cent of the ship's length. The basic type of ship can be taken as the flush-deck type to which various erections have been added, eventually producing the complete superstructure type. A ship may be fitted with a poop, bridge, or forecastle or any combination of the three, separate or combined. The requirements of commerce have evolved many arrangements of superstructure, each type having its own problems in design.

The changing pattern of world trade has produced a demand for fewer, larger and more specialised ships. Economic considerations have increased the speed of ships and engine improvements have made higher speeds possible. All shipping can in very general terms be placed in one of two groups, liners and tramps. The cargo ship which is engaged on a direct and constant trade route or line is in the class of cargo liner. The cargo ship which has an unrestricted service and sails from port to port to pick up freight anywhere is generally referred to as a cargo tramp.

As far as cargo ships are concerned great changes have taken place during the past two decades. Not only have they increased in size and speed but the general cargo carrier is being replaced by specialised ships. These range from 'container' and 'roll-on', 'roll off' ships to the bulk carrier with machinery aft.

Probably the greatest fundamental change in cargo ship layout has been to place the propelling machinery space right aft, as in bulk carrier and oil-tanker practice. With some cargo ships the entire accommodation and navigating bridge space have also been placed right aft, over the machinery space, and thus obtain a clear weather deck which facilitates cargo handling and simplifies the carriage of deck cargo.

Formerly the machinery space in the dry cargo ship was almost invariably placed amidships and there were good reasons for this position; the more important factor being that in the coal-burning ship the fuel had to be carried adjacent to the machinery space and to avoid extreme alterations in trim, as the fuel was consumed, the machinery had to be situated amidships. The advent of oil fuel gave more flexibility in this respect and, also, smaller bunkers facilitated the problem. The use of the amidships portion of the hull for cargo is an obvious improvement, since cargo stowage and handling is much more convenient and thus less time-consuming and costly in terms of stevedoring. Although, of course, the arrangements may not be suitable for all trades.

When the machinery is placed aft the ballast problem is more involved than in the ship with machinery amidships, for unless there is a large ballast tank amidships there is conflict between considerations of trim and the stress in the ballast condition. However, a reasonable compromise is possible by having a midship deep tank fitted which is available for the carriage of cargo as well as ballast. With the fast and fine-lined cargo ships where it would be difficult to install the machinery right aft it is now quite common to place the machinery so that there is one hold aft of the machinery space. This arrangement facilitates problems of trim and strength.

Figure 1 shows the basic flush-deck type of ship as well as some of the arrangements of erections, together with the type having the machinery placed aft.

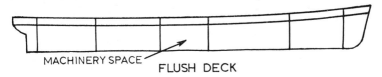

MACHINERY SPACE

FLUSH DECK

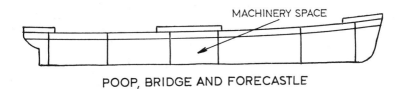

MACHINERY SPACE

POOP, BRIDGE AND FORECASTLE

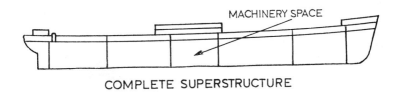

MACHINERY SPACE

COMPLETE SUPERSTRUCTURE

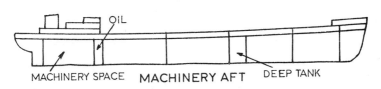

OIL

MACHINERY SPACE MACHINERY AFT DEEP TANK

1 Arrangements of erections and disposition of machinery

Figure 2 shows the midship section of a typical dry cargo ship.

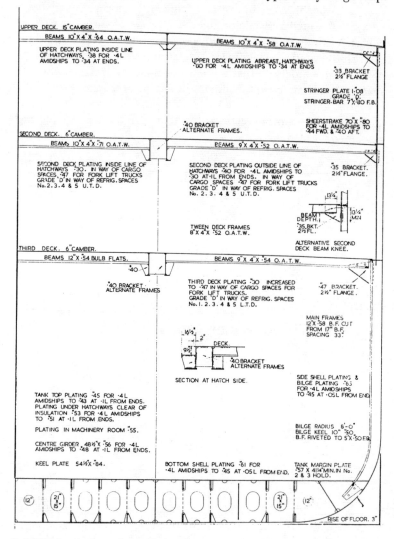

2 Midship section of dry cargo ship

Types of Ships

A brief description is now given of the salient features which characterise the most important types of ships. There are, of course, many variations from these types to suit particular trades.

Oil Tankers

Oil was at first transported in separate tanks aboard ordinary cargo ships and it was not until about 1886 that ships were specially designed for the carriage of oil in bulk. One of these early tankers, the *Looch*, was built by Hawthorn Leslie & Co. in 1886. This vessel had a length of 255 ft, a deadweight of 1650 tons, the power was 1000 IHP and the speed 10 knots. One of the very large tankers at present in service is the *Oriental Dragon*, with a length of 895 ft, a deadweight about 119,000 tons, SHP about 26,000 and a served speed of 17·6 knots.

The growth in the size of oil tankers has been remarkable. In 1948 the average deadweight of tankers built throughout the world was 14,000 tons. In a decade later the average size had doubled. At the time of writing contracts have been signed for tankers of 276,000 tons deadweight and enquiries are being made for tankers of 500,000 tons deadweight.

The oil tanker is one of the few ship types in which the cargo directly rests on the skin of the ship, without the interposition between it and the sea of any other structure such as a double bottom. The carriage of petroleum in bulk necessitates special precautions being taken to meet the difficulties which accompany the transport of such a cargo. The propelling machinery is fitted aft, beneath which is a double bottom space for the accommodation of the oil fuel. The main cargo space in the present-day tanker is subdivided longitudinally by twin oiltight bulkheads and transversely by a number of oiltight bulkheads throughout the length, thus giving several sets of three tanks. To reduce the risk of leakage of oils or vapour into other compartments, a pair of bulkheads which form cofferdams are fitted at each end of the oil cargo range. These cofferdams are well ventilated.

The cargo oil-pumping arrangements are quite extensive, as a number of different grades of oil have to be loaded, transferred from tank to tank and discharged by a pipe network without risk of contamination of one grade by another. There are two cargo-handling pipe arrangements in common use (a) the Ring Main System and (b) Suction Mains. The former consists of a cast-iron pipeline running round the entire cargo tank range; the size depends on the tank capacities and pumping rates desired. The ring main is cross connected by a single pipeline in each of three tanks abreast and thus opposite wing tanks are directly connected. From each crossover there is a branch pipe, having a suction *strum* at its end, led into each of the three abreast tanks. Sluice valves controlled by a handwheel at the upper deck make it possible to isolate the cargo tanks. Any set of tanks may be isolated by means of master valves. The ring main system operates in conjunction with pump rooms situated within the tank range.

The other system in common use consists of suction mains running fore and aft through the cargo tanks. One section main goes to the foremost tank and the others to intermediate positions, each main dealing with a set of tanks which are also interconnected.

Tanks for heavy oils, molasses or other viscid fluids are fitted with heating coils in order that the fluids may be sufficiently liquefied to run freely to the pump suctions.

When oil vapour comes into contact with air an explosive mixture is formed and is dangerous. Consequently adequate provision has to be made to ensure that any foul gas which has accumulated from the oil has a ready means of escape.

A recent development in tankers which has been made possible by the large cubic capacity of the ship is to arrange certain tanks as permanent empty spaces near amidships. This arrangement reduces the still-water bending moment and allows lighter scantlings than would be required if a homogeneous cargo of oil was carried throughout the length of the tank range.

A modern trend is towards concentrating the accommodation and navigating bridge on the poop of the ship. This eliminates the midships house and creates advantages which are of an economic, structural and safety nature.

At one time tankers had a rather unique arrangement in the

connecting gangway between the forecastle and bridge and bridge and poop. These are now eliminated but arrangements are made to give safe access to the forward end of the ship.

Many tankers spend a very high proportion of time at sea. A crude-oil carrier may be up to 330 days each year at sea. This creates problems for those who sail in tankers, and, to attract officers and seamen, accommodation for the entire complement is of the highest order. In many cases single-berth cabins are provided for each member of the crew, and air conditioning is available throughout the accommodation spaces. Amenities include swimming pools, libraries, radios and film shows.

The midship section of a tanker is given in Figure 3 and the profile of a tanker is shown in Figure 4.

Some interesting statistics—shown below—relating to large Japanese tankers have been given in the *United States Naval Institute Proceedings*.

NAME	DEADWEIGHT (Tons)	THICKNESS		COMPLE-MENT	DAYS TO BUILD	COST
		Bottom Shell	Side Shell			
Nissho Maru	132,000	38 mm	25·4 mm	48	329	$105 per ton dwt
Tokyo Maru	150,000	35 mm	23·5 mm	29	228	79·6 do.
Idemitso Maru	205,000	35 mm	24 mm	31	228 est	73·3 do.

The steel plates used in the mammoth tanker *Idemitso Maru* have become thinner although the size has increased and this contributes to savings in steel material. The *Nissho Maru* required a total of 30,000 tons of steel in the construction of the hull and the estimate for the 205,000 tons deadweight tanker is 31,000 tons.

Another feature is the reduction in the complements. The *Nissho Maru*, which is without remote control and automation, required 48 persons, whereas the mammoth tanker requires only 31.

As is shown in the table above, the price went down as the size increased.

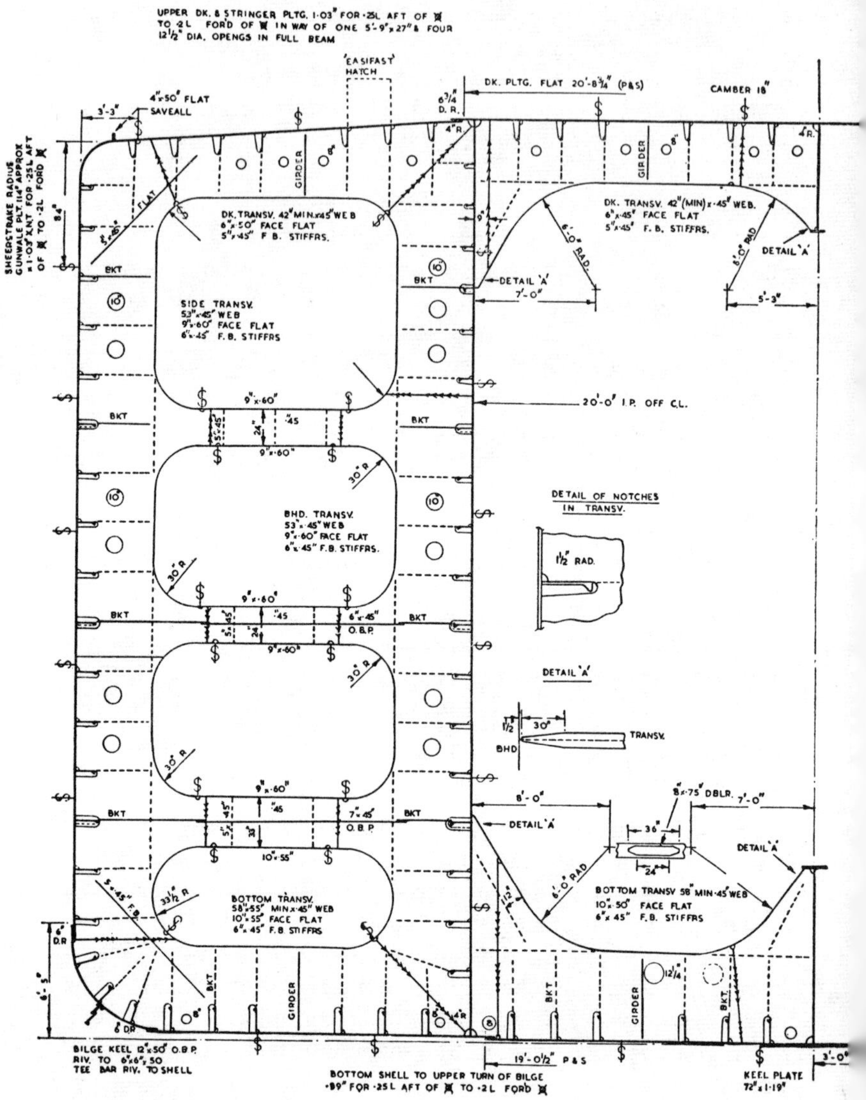

3 Midship section of tanker

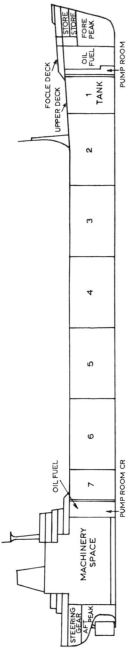

Liquid gas carriers

In the last decade or so specialised ships have been built to carry petroleum gases and other gases in liquid form. The types of liquid gases considered are (1) propane, butane, etc., and (2) methane, ethane, etc. Those in group (1) are carried in spherical or cylindrical tanks at a pressure above atmospheric and at ambient or lower temperatures.

With the increasing demand for these gases cheaper means of transportation and storage were sought. A study of the position showed that it paid to provide refrigerated storage facilities. A French ship was the first ship to have at least part of the cargo refrigerated. There are now a number of ships carrying large quantities of propane in which the cargo is fully refrigerated.

For the liquid gas in group (2) twin transverse bulkheads, double hull and double bottom are required. Water ballast is carried in the double hull and cofferdams. The temperatures for the liquid gases in this group are very low, in the case of methane −258°F, and special materials such as aluminium are used for the cargo tanks. As normal shipbuilding steel is brittle at such temperatures, adequate insulation is of the utmost importance. The hold insulation may be of balsa panels attached to the bottom and sides.

The tanks rest on the bottom insulation and are free to expand and con-

4 Profile of tanker

tract with temperature variation. They are retained in position relative to the ship's structure by suitably placed pitch and roll keys.

It is essential to ensure that any leakage is immediately detected and an effective alarm system is required for this purpose.

An outline profile and midship section of a vessel carrying methane at low temperature are given in Figures 5 and 6.

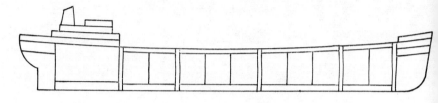

5 Outline profile of vessel carrying methane at low temperature

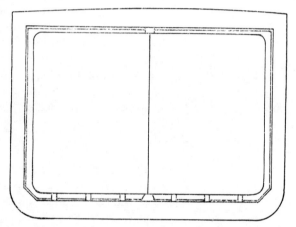

6 Outline midship section of a vessel carrying methane at low temperature

Bulk carriers

Bulk carriers are normally single-deck ships with machinery aft and designed for the carriage of grain, coal or ore cargoes. Several structural arrangements have been adopted, over the years, in this type of ship. The most popular is that with the double bottom sloped up to form a wing tank, and a topside tank extending from the hatch to the side of the ship as shown in Figure 7.

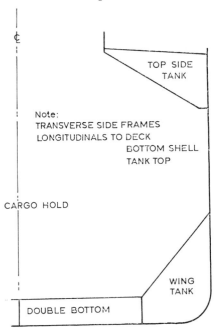

7 Midship section of bulk carrier

The solid-bulk cargo is one which can be loaded into a ship's hold by gravity and discharged by grabs, conveyor system or, as in the case of grain, by suction. Grain is part way between a solid and a liquid cargo and has some of the properties of both. Specific regulations are laid down by International Convention which govern the carriage of grain.

Where ships are designed for the carriage of iron-ore special provision is made for the reception in the holds of this very heavy cargo. These vessels generally have two longitudinal bulkheads, as in a tanker, the ore being carried in the centre portion between these and on top of a deep double bottom. An outline section of an ore carrier is shown in Figure 8. In general these vessels have longitudinal framing to the double bottom, shell and deck. The most recent adaptation is the combined ore and oil carrier and in this the main structure of the ship has to be in accordance with the ore standard and the bulkheads have to be equivalent to the oil tanker standard. The transverse section of this type is

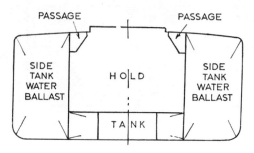

8 Outline section of ore carrier

shown in Figure 9. For the protection of the crew, underdeck passages are provided as shown in the figure. Since oil is carried, there is a cofferdam between the passage and the tanks.

The bulk carrier is now available to carry a wide range of cargoes such as sugar, newsprint, cement, bauxite, etc., and the structure of the ship must be appropriate to the most onerous trade in which it is likely to be engaged. So far the bulk carrier has lagged behind the oil tanker as far as size is concerned, but this has been due to the dimensional limitations of docks and harbours. Unlike the oil tanker, a bulk carrier must enter a port to be unloaded; it cannot unload at the end of a jetty extending into deep water with anything like the ease of the corresponding loading or unloading of the tanker.

Refrigerated cargo ships

These vessels are specially equipped with refrigerating machinery and insulated holds for the carriage of meat or other perishable cargo. Due to the depth of insulation the cubic capacity of the cargo spaces is quite substantially reduced. Some classes of cargo such as mutton and pork can be frozen hard without damage to their food value; others such as beef cargoes generally arrive in better condition if only chilled.

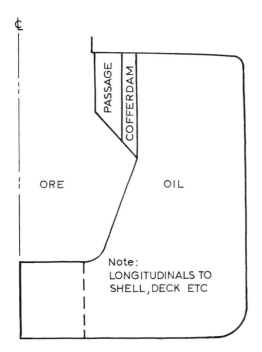

9 Outline section of combined ore and oil carrier

Chilled beef is hung from hooks and chains and there is about 1 ft clear space below the meat to permit circulation of air. The height of storage of frozen meat should not exceed 20 ft to avoid crushing lower tiers.

Bananas are transported in bins and are stacked in tiers, two tiers placed vertically and one horizontally.

Passenger liners

The requirements of the various services on the regular passenger routes differ appreciably. In the case of a ship which is predominantly passenger-carrying, the space available for cargo is of minor importance. In such ships the comfort of passengers is of prime importance and the amenities provided must be extensive and excellent. In addition to the usual public rooms, it is essential to make provision for cinemas, swimming pools, shops, etc., and the greatest possible extent of deck space. Many passenger ships engage in cruising during the off-season and in certain cases this may mean that a portion of the accommodation may have to be interchangeable.

The number of large passenger liners is being reduced, due mainly to air competition, and many of these ships are making ends meet with cruising. It is unlikely that there will be any boom in the building of this class of ship. Just after the second world war the United Kingdom had a near-monopoly of large passenger-ship building. Italy has produced a number, while a few have come from the shipyards of the USA, France, the Netherlands and Belgium. It is significant that Japan, Germany and Sweden, which with the UK top the tables of world tonnage production, have done very little in this market.

When built in 1948 the Cunarder *Caronia* was the first large British passenger liner to be designed and built specifically for year-round cruising.

A notable feature of passenger liners is the extent of built-up superstructure. In 1894 the Merchant Shipping Act did not permit passengers to be carried on more than two decks. This restriction was removed in 1906 by an amendment to the Act to the effect that passengers could not be carried on more than one deck below the waterline; no mention is made of passengers above that deck. The addition of several tiers of superstructures creates problems of strength and stability. A considerable contribution to the solution of these problems is in the adoption of aluminium alloy for the superstructures. This makes it possible to accept greater strains and displacements than would be possible with steel. Aluminium superstructures are, in general terms, about half the weight of the corresponding steel superstructures and consequently this eases the stability problem.

Most passenger liners are fitted with anti-rolling fins and in a number of cases are also provided with bow propellers to assist in docking and manœuvring. The problem of excessive pitching has still to be solved and no doubt this will be achieved in time.

Two important contributions to passenger-ship design are the advances in marine engineering which has enabled a reduction in the size of the machinery space; the installation of air conditioning which has extended the adoption of inside cabins. The propelling machinery has traditionally been located about amidships, for probably the same reasons as has been indicated for cargo ships. There is a trend towards placing the machinery right aft. This gives a clear space for accommodation amidships but eliminates the sheltered passenger deck space at the aft end and also creates the problem of obtaining a suitable trim without inducing excessive hogging stresses. In certain ships, notably the *Southern Cross* and the *Canberra*, the advantages of machinery aft have overruled the disadvantages.

Cross-channel ships

Cross-channel services, as they are generically termed, form the link, in general, between railheads, the sea routes being planned so that connecting rail services are available from the terminals at one—or both—ends of the passage.

Cross-channel passenger ships usually have a speed in excess of 20 knots and are often looked upon as an Atlantic liner in miniature. The two types have much in common, since both are required to carry passengers and small quantities of highly freighted goods quickly from terminal port to terminal port in a minimum of time, and with as rapid a turn round in port as possible.

Cross-channel ships operate under all weather conditions across the world's busiest shipping lanes; for example, the density of traffic through the English Channel averages one ship every two minutes. They enter and leave port without the aid of pilots or tugs and in peak periods often make eight crossings per day. Turning a ship in a small harbour or narrow river is a slow operation and time is saved by berthing stern first whenever possible. The high speed necessitates a large power requirement for propulsion. Most ships of this type have twin screws for greater manœuvrability. Bow rudders to assist when manœuvring when

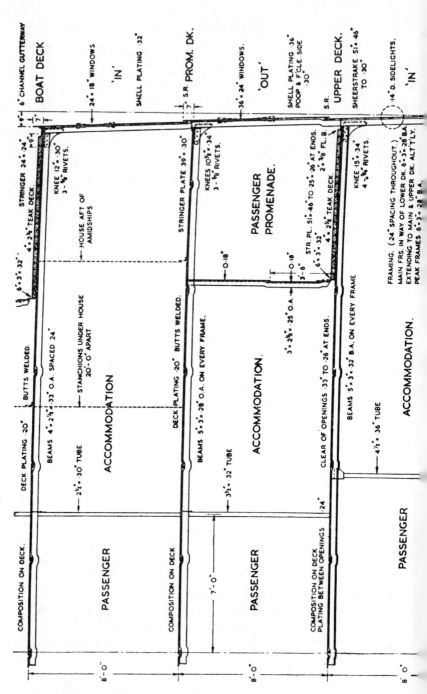

10 Midship section of cross-Channel ship

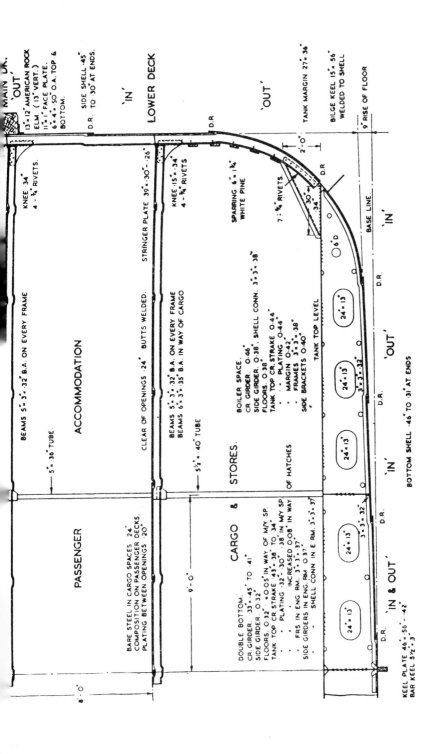

going astern are a common feature and recent practice is to install a propulsion unit in an athwartship tunnel forward in order to provide sideways thrust for rapid turning. Stabilisers are invariably fitted to the passenger ships. As these vessels berth frequently and manœuvre alongside quay walls permanent fendering is a necessity. The fendering is usually of elm, square in section about 12 in side bolted between flat plates welded to the shell and faced with a flat bar secured to the timber by spikes. The fendering is arranged at heights above the waterline to suit quay facilities.

Cross-channel passenger ships fall into three classes as (a) ships on daylight routes, (b) ships on night routes, and (c) ships which run alternatively by day or by night. The problem of design for either (a) or (b) is much simpler than for (c), where the space available must be used to the limit and difficulties of compromise frequently arise.

The passenger ship designed for day service has large public rooms in lounges, restaurant and/or cafeteria, smoke rooms and bars, arranged generally on three or four enclosed decks. In fine weather the majority of passengers, quite naturally, like to be on the open deck and thus it is essential to provide as much open deck space as possible. In addition to the passenger ships there are train ferries and vehicular ferries. Some of the passenger ships also have provision for the carriage of motor vehicles. In the passenger-vehicular ferries the below deck space is laid out as a garage, with the vehicle deck running the entire length of the ship and fitted with turntables. On the deck over the garage space and above, the passenger accommodation is arranged. In general these vessels operate as a stern-loading drive-on, drive-off type of ship in which there is a large watertight door, in some instances hydraulically operated, set into the stern. The door is hinged on its lower edge so that when lowered it forms a ramp for loading and unloading the vehicles. The midship section of a typical cross-channel ship is shown in Figure 10.

The modern ferry is a ship to cater for three dimensions—passengers, motor cars, and cargo packed in containers or bulk units. All three are transported in complete isolation from one another on different decks. Comfort, good food, drinks, duty-free shops and amusement aboard are the keynote of modern ferries for the passengers and rapid door-to-door delivery the aim of the cargo exporters. New ferries, in general, are one class, as in this way space is saved by not having to duplicate public rooms and facilities as for a two-class ship. This simplifies design and keeps down building cost.

Container ships

Ever since the days of ancient Egypt goods loaded into and out of ships have been lifted up, moved across and lowered down. In general the idea of doors in the side or ends that come down to form ramps was not adopted until the second world war made it essential to land goods on open beaches. This was the beginning of a revolution which has brought roll-on, roll-off (RO-RO) through doors and over ramps and the container system. It is hoped by the container system to make savings in packing costs, speed up loading and unloading and offer increased protection against pilferage, damage and deterioration.

Specialised service of this kind requires specialised ships and these are being built. Standard containers are stacked in cellular holds and on the deck. The entire cargo space in such a container ship is taken up by sectionalised holds containing cellular compartments. The development of the container-ship concept has been rapid and will make a great impact upon port development. The driving force of a fully integrated container service is such that nothing around it can remain the same. Much more space will be required around each berth and existing cranes will probably become obsolete.

Tugs

Tugs are looked upon as the 'maids of all work' of the merchant fleets of the world, and the services expected from them are many and varied. Generally tugs may be classified according to their duties as follows:
(a) River, (b) Harbour, (c) Coastal, and (d) Ocean-going and Salvage.

The development of particular types of tugs to suit varying

c

services and port conditions and the availability of a variety of propelling units has resulted in tug design becoming a specialised branch of naval architecture. The requirements for each class of tug are stability under all conditions, manœuvrability, and adequate towing power. Whilst all other ships are powered solely for themselves, the efficiency of the tug as such is dependent on the amount of power the vessel can transmit through a tow-rope to some other vessel. Some medium-sized harbour tugs have powers of 1500 BHP and a pull of up to 25 tons.

Next to the ability to tow successfully a tug must be manœuvrable and to this end much research work has been carried out. One arrangement is to have the propeller encased in a swivelling ring which acts as the rudder; this is the Kort nozzle propulsion. Another form is the Voith Schneider propeller where the blades are vertical. The operation of tugs in sheltered waters is not without its dangers. The main risk confronting the ship-handling tug is that of being dragged sideways by the towline until the vessel heels over and possibly capsizes. To prevent this provision is generally made for the towline to be released speedily, such as by a towing hook that releases under a predetermined load.

The ship-handling tug quite frequently does not actually tow its charges but helps them to steer in the correct channel and the larger ship propels itself. The head tug uses the tow-hook, which is rigidly attached to the structure and at the same time free to swing through a large angle. For the tug holding the stern, the tow-rope is attached to a samson post fitted on the centre line of the tug just abaft the stem. Side samson posts are also provided for the purpose of lashing craft alongside.

In the ocean-going and salvage tugs the main characteristics are power, seagoing qualities, radius of action and displacement. Towing conditions are very different in ocean service from that in the other tug range. At sea in bad weather a long tow-rope is essential; breakage of the tow-rope is brought about by shocks due to varying speeds of the tug and the vessel being towed due to weather conditions. A towing winch is an effective means of overcoming such difficulties. These winches take a predetermined load, and if this is suddenly exceeded the winch automatically pays out wire; when the excessive load is relaxed the winch takes in the wire. All ocean-going tugs carry a considerable amount of salvage equipment, including salvage pumps, fixed and flexible hose, fire pumps, monitors, and fire foam equipment. A comprehensive range of navigational equipment is provided as well as clusters of floodlights and a searchlight.

The midship section of a tug is shown in Figure 11 and the general arrangement of a harbour tug in Figure 11a.

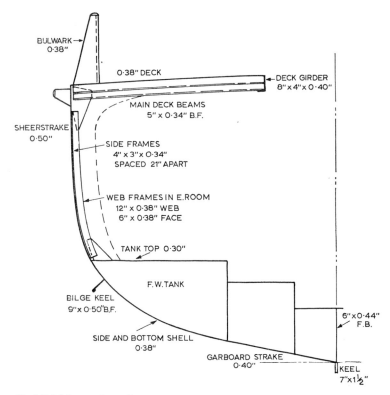

11 Midship section of a tug

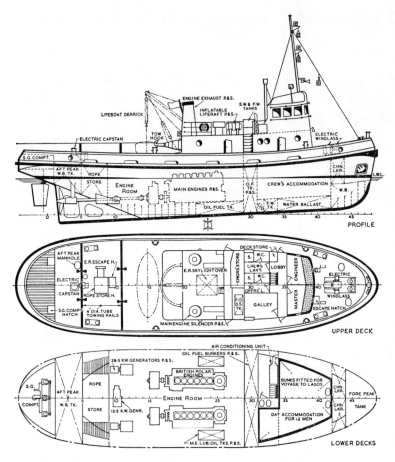

11a General arrangement of a harbour tug

Trawlers

The trawler presents many problems that do not arise in any other class of seagoing vessel. The cargo ship is given a definite cargo to take from or to some specified port. The trawler has to proceed to a distant fishing ground, commence trawling, take the catch on board, gut, clean, and stow it, and then proceed to the home port.

The cargo has to be sought, brought home in good marketable condition, and then sold by auction. For the conventional side trawler the main characteristics are a deep draught aft to ensure the ship will trawl effectively in heavy weather, a freeboard which is the best compromise between the maximum range of stability and ease of handling the trawl overside, and adequate power to tow the trawl in rough weather. As the cargo is perishable, speed is desirable for the return voyage to the market.

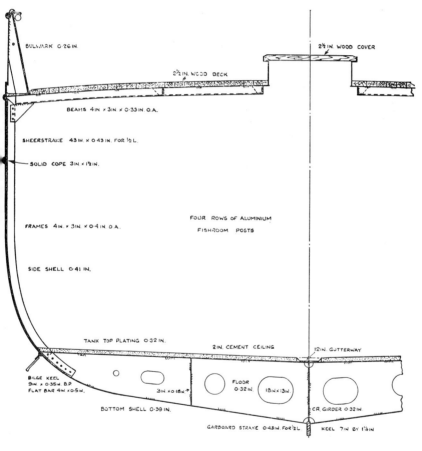

12 Midship section of a trawler

The quality of the fish landed depends not only upon the care with which the fish is cleaned and stowed but also upon the condition of the fish room. The fish hold is divided longitudinally and transversely into spaces each about 4 ft with a centre passage of about the same width. The shelves and pound boards are of wood or alloy. Ice and fish are placed alternately in layers on top of the shelves. The shelves distribute the load, avoiding excessive pressure and crushing of the bottom layer of fish. The fishing fleet is constantly being improved with more efficient methods of fishing and the introduction of freezing equipment to preserve the catch. In this way the stay in the fishing grounds can be lengthened to an extent depending upon the size of the fish hold.

Stern-fishing trawlers are now being extensively used and it is claimed that by this method the time and work of bringing gear and catch aboard, emptying the nets and putting the gear back into the sea is reduced. It is also claimed that conditions are made safer for the crew.

A new type of ship has been evolved; this is the self-trawling, stern-operated fish factory. The net is brought up a chute at the stern on to the fish-landing deck. The fish is then dropped through hatches into fish pounds on the factory deck below. Here the catch is sorted and prepared by heading, skinning, gutting and filleting machinery prior to being sent to the freezing plant. After the special quick-freezers the fish is packed in cartons and then placed in deep-freeze holds. Cod livers are processed and the oil pumped into storage tanks. The offal is dealt with by a fish-meal plant. There is thus no waste and the entire process is carried out on the ship.

The midship section of a trawler and arrangement plan of a stern trawler are shown in Figures 12 and 13.

Ice-breakers

The hazards which ice presents to shipping fall into two classes, that presented by icebergs and that presented by sea ice. The former is more haphazard and generally by far the more dangerous, but the latter, which constitutes more than 95 per cent of all floating ice, affects to a much greater extent the construction of

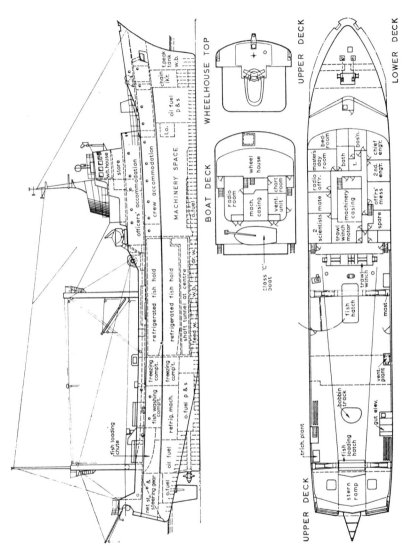

13 General arrangement of a stern trawler

ships. Almost all icebergs are derived from glaciers. A moderate-sized iceberg will weigh 30 million tons and their great bulk allows them to drift far into warmer waters before melting. As approximately eight-ninths of an iceberg lies below the sea surface, they are more sensitive to currents than to winds.

In the early spring of each year the current which runs down the west side of Baffin Bay carries a procession of icebergs, which spread out into the Atlantic shipping lanes, and it was such an iceberg that sank the *Titanic* in 1912. The International Ice Patrol, created because of this disaster, and the development of navigational aids such as radar, have greatly reduced this hazard to shipping.

Sea ice, which is just the frozen surface of the sea, is kept moving by winds and currents and breaks into floes. The floes are encountered in all sizes up to 10 miles long and 12 ft thick. The dangers of navigation in sea ice are not so much from striking individual floes but from the possibility of the ship being trapped in a large area of ice and then subjected to crushing pressures.

For a number of northern countries the main approaches by sea are frozen for a considerable proportion of the year. In some countries, notably Finland and other Baltic countries, navigation through ice cannot be avoided and it is in such conditions that the ice-breaker functions.

The first ship known to be expressly built to keep navigation open in winter was the *Polhem*, built in Sweden in 1857. The Russians had a ship built in 1870 to keep open the port of Kronstadt and in 1871 the Germans built the appropriately named *Eisbrecher*, which operated between Hamburg and Cuxhaven. Since that time the ice-breaker has been developed as a distinct type of ship.

By reason of the work they have to perform, ice-breakers are entirely different from any other type of ship, and an important characteristic is extreme strength. The hull must be able to withstand not only the actual shock of striking but also the possible danger of being squeezed in the ice. Ice-breakers clear a passage through the ice by steaming at it, mounting on it and then crushing a portion of it by their weight. To accomplish this the vessel has a very strong and steep rising forefoot or stem which permits the ship to slide up on to the ice. The frames of the vessel are spaced very close together and the shell plating is unusually thick. To further strengthen the hull against ice pressure a strake of plating is fitted about 6 ft broad and $1\frac{1}{2}$ in thick along the waterline. Some ice-breakers have a propeller or propellers in the bow and this indeed is a feature of most Baltic ships of this type. The purpose of this is to assist the crushing action when the vessel mounts on the ice; by giving the water under the ice a sternward motion, it is robbed of its support, and consequently can be easier crushed. The bow propeller also performs another function by washing away broken ice from the fore end and thus reducing friction between the ice and the sides of the ship.

With regard to the propelling machinery the ice-breaker has kept pace with progress from steam reciprocating to the now widely favoured diesel electric. There is, of course, the nuclear-powered *Lenin*; this ship has turbo-electric machinery of 44,000 hp, a speed of 18 knots, and can move continuously through solid pack ice 6 ft thick.

Accommodation on ice-breakers is of a very high standard and every possible provision is made for the comfort of the ship's complement.

A typical ice-breaker is shown in Figure 14.

Dredgers

A very important auxiliary to navigation is in the dredger, in all its types. The prosperity of a port depends to some extent upon the navigability of its approaches. Dredgers and their auxiliaries are designed to remove material from the bed of a channel and deposit it elsewhere. The procedure depends upon the nature of the material to be removed. A sand or mud bottom will require treatment different to that of stiff clay and different again from that required by a hard rocky bottom.

Dredgers fall into various categories and the three main types are bucket, suction, and grab. All these types may be self-propelling or non-self-propelling and hopper or non-hopper. The latter terms simply mean that they either discharge the spoil into hoppers alongside, or into hoppers contained within the hull structure.

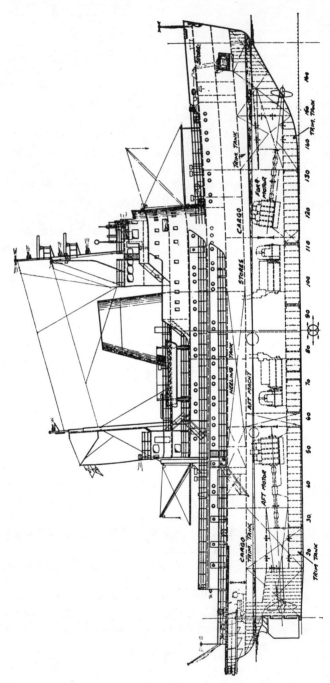

14 General arrangement of an ice-breaker

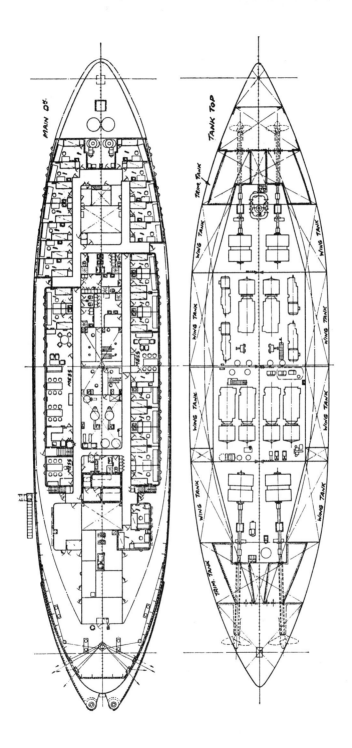

In the bucket or ladder dredger the buckets are attached to an endless chain working over an arm, the outboard end of which can be lowered to suit the required depth for dredging. The buckets pass through an open well situated in the fore or after end of the vessel. The spoil brought up by the buckets is discharged through a shoot leading into the hopper of the dredger or into a separate hopper moored alongside. It is quite common to engage a fairly frequent service of self-propelled hoppers to take the dredged material away and deposit it at sea upon the recognised spoil grounds.

Where the material to be removed is mud or sand the suction type dredger is the most suitable. Instead of the bucket ladder a pipe is used which is attached to a suction or centrifugal pump. The outboard end can be lowered and the material drawn up and discharged into a hopper or pumped through other portable pipes and deposited on adjacent land.

In the grab dredger the material is excavated by means of a grab operated by a crane mounted on the dredger. The crane may be arranged to grab over the side or over the bow or stern, and discharge the spoil into a hopper. The jaws of the grab are open when lowered and are closed by the action of the engine on the chain attached to the grab.

For the removal of rock a special vessel is required which has a ram-weight having a hard-alloy steel point and weighing up to 15 tons. The rock is broken up by pounding with this weight, which is raised by a winch and allowed to drop under gravity. The rock can also be broken up using explosives and the broken rock removed by a bucket or grab dredger.

Hopper barges

As already stated, dredgers frequently work in conjunction with hopper barges which carry the spoil to a suitable dumping area. In these barges the hold bottom is fitted with hinged doors which, when opened, permit the spoil to fall out under gravity; the doors can then be closed. The doors are controlled by chains passing over sheaves and then led to winches. The spaces on each side of the hopper compartments are left empty to provide sufficient buoyancy. The section of a hopper barge is shown in Figure 15. Typical dredgers are shown in Figures 16, 16a and 17.

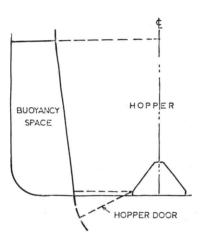

15 Section of hopper barge

16 Bucket dredger

16a Close-up view of buckets

17 Suction hopper-dredger *Abbotsgrange*

Cable ships

Cable ships are, by reason of their duties, complex and specialised ships. One of the unusual features of cable ships as compared with other merchant-ship types is that they usually discharge their cargo during the voyage instead of at the destination.

It is of interest to consider some of the features and characteristics of vessels designed and constructed for the laying, repair and maintenance of submarine telegraph cables. As there are long distances of cable to maintain and the ship will be obliged to remain at sea for protracted periods, it is essential to have a large fuel capacity and a strong seaworthy hull to withstand the vagaries of the weather. A clear deck space forward as a working platform is essential. The internal hull arrangement must be such as to enable long lengths of cable to be carried. The cable is stored in cylindrical tanks and coiled on steel cones built up from the base of the tank. These cones are fitted with a special arrangement known as a crinoline to prevent the cable kinking as it is payed out. For paying out and picking up cables a special type of winch, together with sheaves or rollers over which the cable can run, dynamometers, deck leads to guide the cable to the machines, must be fitted.

An important characteristic of cable ships is to be able to manœuvre at slow speeds, since the vessel must maintain station over the line of cable when either picking up or paying out.

A brief description of the method of operation of a cable ship in carrying out cable-repair duties is now given. Electrical measurements by engineers ashore at both ends of the cable enable the approximate position of the fault to be determined. This information is passed to the ship and a marker buoy is dropped at the spot and the vessel proceeds to grapple for the cable by passing across its route until it is located. The cable is then raised from the sea bed to the bow sheaves by the winch and tested by sending a signal through it in each direction to the shore stations. The direction in which the fault lies is, of course, indicated by the failure of one of the shore stations to reply. The ship then travels slowly along the line of cable towards the fault, hauling the cable aboard at the same time until the fault is located. The faulty section is then replaced by a new section which is spliced in and tested, and the cable is then returned to the sea bed.

A typical cable ship is shown in Figure 18.

18 Cable-laying ship *Mercury*

THE HYDROFOIL VESSEL AND HOVERCRAFT

Hydrofoil craft

The prototype of the hydrofoil vessel was built and patented in 1891 by C. A. de Lambert. These vessels, poised on 'sea-legs', can attain speeds up to about 60 knots. The hydrofoil craft does not, as generally thought, skim the water on the foils. The main foil or foils travel totally or partially submerged, attached to struts which are in turn connected to the hull. The main objective is to get the hull over the waves instead of through them. The development of the high-speed diesel and the arrival of gas turbines have made it possible for the hydrofoil craft, in certain restricted waters, to be a useful form of transport.

There are a number of designs of hydrofoil craft and the foil arrangements are in four groups: submerged, hoop, ladder and skimming, as shown diagrammatically in Figure 19.

For prime movers there are, as stated above, two types—diesels or gas turbines. Diesels have proved satisfactory but are somewhat limited in maximum power. The gas turbine would appear to be the answer for the large and very fast hydrofoil craft.

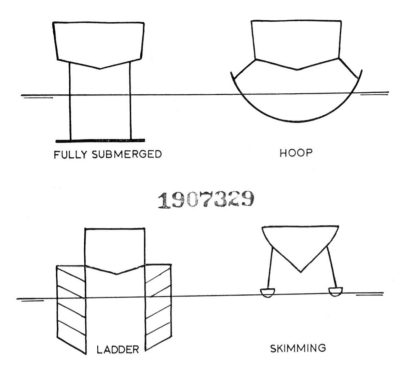

FULLY SUBMERGED   HOOP

1907329

LADDER   SKIMMING

19 Foil arrangements

Of the three methods of obtaining thrust—water propellers, air-screw propellers and water jets—the water propeller is favoured, but there arises the problem of cavitation. Cavitation occurs when the water flowing over the upper surface of the foil or propeller blade leaves the metal face and creates a space which is almost a vacuum. The effect of this is to damage the foils and the propellers by the impact of water when the cavities collapse.

Hydrofoil craft can move at high speed without causing a big wash and can be exempted from the speed limits normally imposed in restricted waterways. Hydrofoil travel is comfortable and in crowded areas are very desirable for their good manœuvrability and low noise level. Figure 20 shows the *Guia*, a hydrofoil built under Lloyd's Register survey for Hong Kong. The maximum speed is about 38 knots. This craft carries 124 passengers.

20 Hydrofoil

Hovercraft

An advanced high-speed marine craft with considerable potential is now in restricted operation. This is the hovercraft.

After a relatively short period of development, hovercraft, or air-cushion craft, have demonstrated an ability to operate in moderate sea conditions and have reached the stage of being able to carry fare-paying passengers.

As yet the hovercraft is by no means an all-weather craft, since there are limitations on the height of the waves in which it can operate comfortably. Progress with hovercraft has been slow; tentative ideas were proposed by De Laval in 1883 but with little practical result. A practical means was given by C. S. Cockerell in the 1950s and the operational hovercraft became feasible. Since then considerable theoretical work on the subject has been carried out and several hovercraft have been built.

The hovercraft has yet to be accepted as a fully practical commercial ferry craft. Noise and spray are serious objections, but in spite of this experimental services have shown that hovercraft have public appeal. Over pack ice or swamp the hovercraft or air-cushion vehicle has no competitors.

Figure 21 gives an artist's impression of the 160-ton SRN 4

21 160-ton SRN 4 Hovercraft

Hovercraft by the British Hovercraft Corporation Ltd. This craft has an overall length of 130 ft 2 in, breadth 76 ft 10 in and a maximum speed of 77 knots. The power plant consists of four Bristol Siddeley gas-turbine engines each rated at 3400 SHP maximum. The all-passenger version can accommodate 600 people seated. The first service between Ramsgate and Calais is expected to commence in the spring of 1968.

II · NOTES ON SHIP CONSTRUCTION

The fundamental constructive features in a ship design must be such as to enable the vessel to preserve an intact hull that will have sufficient strength, by a suitable disposition of the material in the shell, decks and bulkheads, to withstand all the stresses and dangers that may be encountered in the service or trade in which the ship is engaged. In addition to this it is essential that the ship remains in a condition of seaworthiness.

Under service conditions a ship is continually meeting stresses of varying character brought about by the condition of the sea, wind pressure and the disposition of the cargo.

Development of the structure of a ship has been influenced by three closely allied considerations:

(a) eliminating internal obstructions so as to give clear holds for the stowage and working of cargo.

(b) reducing the weight of the ship by the most efficient disposition of the structural material.

(c) ensuring that the hull structure is of adequate strength to withstand the forces of the sea.

The strains to which ships are subjected may be divided into two classes:

(1) Structural strains: these affect the structure of the ship considered as a whole and are those which (a) tend to cause the ship

to bend in a fore and aft direction, (b) tend to change the transverse form of the ship.

(2) Local strains: these affect particular parts of the ship, such
as panting strains and strains due to local concentration of weights.

As a simple illustration of the meaning of stress and strain
assume a steel rod of circular cross-section of area A and of length
l as shown in Figure 22. Assume one end fixed at F and a force P

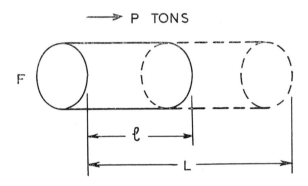

22 Stress and strain

applied along the length of the rod. Immediately the force is
applied the material begins to alter shape, in this case the rod
lengthens to say L. As long as the external force does not exceed
the internal resistance there will be no permanent alteration in the
form of the bar. The point where on the force being released the
material returns to the original shape and if stretched beyond this
point permanent alteration of form takes place is referred to as
the 'elastic limit' or 'limit of proportionality'.

Stress is the intensity of the load which tends to alter the shape
of the rod and is expressed in tons per square inch.

$$Stress = \frac{P}{A} \text{ where P is force applied in tons}$$

and A is cross-sectional area in inches.[2]

Strain is the magnitude of the alteration to the shape of the rod

produced by the action of stress. It is measured by the extension
or contraction per unit length in the direction the stress is applied.

$$\text{Stretch or extension} = L - l$$
$$\text{Strain} = \frac{L - l}{l}$$

The ratio of stress to strain—within the limits of elasticity—is a
constant quantity and is known as the

$$\text{Modulus of elasticity} = \frac{\text{stress}}{\text{strain}}$$

The force as applied in Figure 22 tends to pull the rod apart and is
termed a 'tensile' stress; if the force is applied in the opposite
direction the stress is 'compressive' and if applied perpendicular
to the length of the rod it is a 'shearing' stress.

Suppose a bar of steel to be supported at its ends with a load (W)
applied at the middle of its length, as shown in Figure 23. The

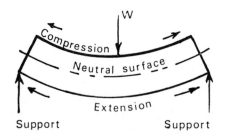

Support   Support

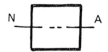

Cross-section at
middle of length
note:
N.A.=Neutral axis

23 Neutral axis

tendency will be for the bar to sag in the middle. The upper
surface of this bar will be in compression and the lower surface
will be in tension. Between these two surfaces there must be a

layer of the bar unaffected by either compression or tension. This layer or 'neutral surface', as it is termed, passes through the centre of gravity of the section of the bar. In the cross-section of the bar shown in Figure 23 the line drawn at the neutral surface is called the 'neutral axis'.

The extent of elongation and compression of any layer is directly proportional to its distance from the neutral axis (N.A.). Thus as the upper and lower layers of the bar are the most strained, being farthest from the neutral axis, the stresses are a maximum at the upper and lower edges.

A ship may be regarded as a large beam or girder subject to bending in a fore-and-aft direction. The weight of the ship is unevenly distributed throughout the length, while the buoyancy or support from the water is constant in proportion to the volume of the ship immersed. There is, therefore, in different parts of the

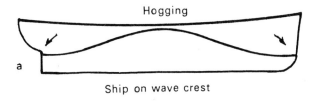

Hogging

Ship on wave crest

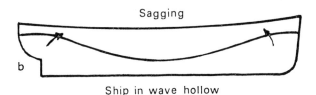

Sagging

Ship in wave hollow

24 Hogging and sagging

hull, an excess of buoyancy over weight, and in other sections an excess of weight over buoyancy. In Figure 24a the ship is assumed to be on the crest of a wave. In this condition the stresses exerted on the ship are the result of excess of weight at the ends and excess of buoyancy amidships. Consequently there is a tendency for the ends to droop relatively to the middle. This is termed 'hogging'.

In Figure 24b the ship is assumed to be in the trough of a wave when the stresses acting on the ship are opposite to those referred to above. In this condition there is an excess of weight amidships and an excess of buoyancy at the ends. Thus there is a tendency for the middle to droop relatively to the ends. This is termed 'sagging'.

As already stated, a ship may be compared to a beam and the following illustrates how the material should be disposed to best withstand the bending strains. Assume a beam supported at the ends and with a load (W) at the middle as in Figure 25. The

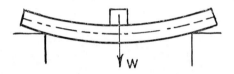

25 Beam loaded at middle of length

maximum stress produced when the beam bends depends on the form of the cross-section of the beam. For convenience assume a cross-sectional area of 16 sq in and disposed in three ways as shown in Figure 26.

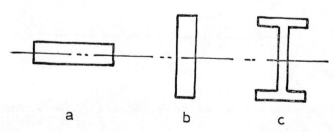

a   b   c

26 Form of cross-section

(a) 8 in wide and 2 in deep.

(b) 2 in wide and 8 in deep.

(c) 8 in deep with flanges top and bottom 5 in wide. The flanges and web being 1 in thick.

It can be shown that the maximum bending moments which these beams can stand within the elastic limit are as follows:

If (a) is taken as 1 then (b) is 4 and (c) is $6\frac{5}{8}$. This shows that to make the beam stronger to resist bending the material should be disposed away from the neutral axis. Beam (c) has $6\frac{5}{8}$ times the strength of (a) against bending, although the sectional area of each is the same. Thus in a ship to resist bending strains the material of the structure should be disposed away from the neutral axis.

In hogging the upper portions of the ship are in tension and the lower portion in compression. In sagging the upper portions are in compression and the lower in tension. The parts of the structure that are useful in resisting these hogging and sagging strains are the decks, shell plating, inner bottom and longitudinal framing.

The stresses at the ends of the ship are not so great as those amidships, so that in disposing the material throughout the length the scantlings or thicknesses of the plating, etc., are reduced gradually towards the ends.

There are also stresses due to the vessel rolling among waves. Such movements tend to produce distortion and to prevent deformation of the transverse form the connections of the decks with the sides and the main framing at the bilge should be well strengthened. Transverse bulkheads are valuable in resisting the tendency to change the transverse form.

Local stresses are felt in many parts of the ship and some of these are as follows:

Panting stresses

These are brought about by fluctuating pressures upon the immersed hull at the ends when a ship is among waves and the tendency is to make the plating work in and out or 'pant'. The forward end especially is subject to severe blows from the sea and special attention is paid to this part by fitting deep floors, extra tiers of beams and stringers.

Pounding stresses

Ships of full form are also subject to several local stresses on the bottom framing and plating forward when driven into head seas. Pounding, or as it is sometimes termed 'slamming', is most likely to occur when the ship is in ballast condition, particularly if there is a large trim by the stern. Additional stiffening in the form of thick bottom plating and deep plate floors are used to combat these stresses.

Stresses caused by vibration

All parts of the hull girder have their natural periods of vibration and it is only when the period of the moving parts of the propelling machinery synchronises with that of the ship girder that vibration may become serious. Most ships are practically free from vibration when the machinery is running at certain speeds.

Local vibration may be the result of weakness or lack of continuity in the ship's structure and when this is the case it is necessary to stiffen the structure.

The foregoing is an outline of the principal considerations which control the disposition of the structural material in a cargo or passenger ship.

There are, as the result of experience, certain permissible stresses and in a ship design these are not allowed to be exceeded. Extensive calculations for weight, buoyancy, load, shearing forces and bending moments are carried out and plotted as curves; these, together with the calculation for the section modulus or modulus of resistance $\left[\dfrac{I}{Y} \right]$ are used in the preparation of the final design. Detailed reference to these various calculations will not be made in this work, as they are beyond the knowledge required by the non-technical personnel.

The midship section of a ship, which is a transverse section at the position of mid-length, indicates the scantlings or sizes of the material it is intended to use in the structure of the hull.

Figures 2, 3, 10, 11, 12, 27 show the midship sections of several types of ships. The type of framing, transverse or longitudinal, is clearly indicated.

Material and tests

The steel used in the construction of ships and their machinery intended to be classed with a Classification Society must conform to the prescribed tests. For shipbuilding purposes the plates and various sections used are generally of mild steel having a tensile strength within 26 to 32 tons per sq in. This material can be rolled, forged or welded and meets most of the requirements of the shipbuilding industry. There are various processes used in the manufacture of mild steel but the open hearth is the process generally favoured for the manufacture of steel for ship construction. The use of the electric-furnace process is steadily increasing. A disadvantage of ordinary mild steel is that at low temperatures it is somewhat lacking in notch-toughness. This means that a fracture, once started, may spread rapidly across a plate until it meets some effective barrier. Such a barrier or 'crack arrester' is a riveted seam. In riveted ships, fractures rarely, if ever, travel across a seam into the adjacent plate. In a welded ship a welded seam offers no such resistance and a plate fracture may extend rapidly with serious results. The tendency to notch-brittleness increases with increase in plate thickness. Consequently it is now the practice, in welded ships, to require that the plating of the main strength members, when over a specified thickness, shall be of steels possessing a higher notch-toughness than ordinary mild steel. In large tankers, for example, it is required that a number of the deck and shell seams be riveted, or, alternatively, steel of still higher notch-toughness be used.

At one time each Classification Society had its own requirements for these special steels, but as a result of unification of their requirements there are now only five different qualities of steel used in merchant shipbuilding.

The prescribed tests and inspection of the steel, already referred

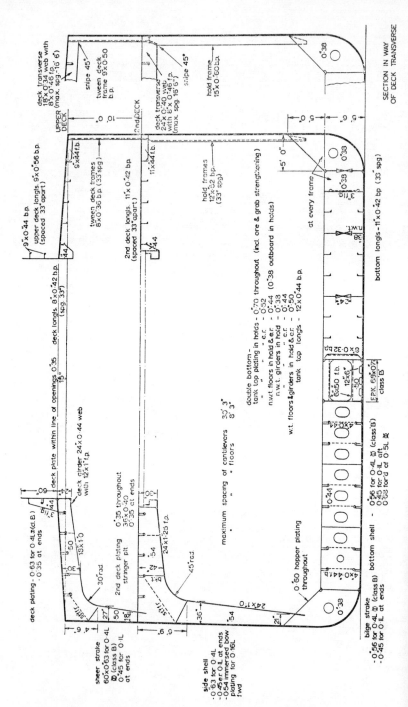

27 Midship section of cargo ship

to, are carried out by the Society surveyors at the place of manufacture prior to dispatch and they select the test pieces which are tested in their presence.

The following is a summary of the tests required by Lloyd's Register for mild steel.

A tensile and a bend test are required to be made from one piece rolled from each 'cast'.

Where impact tests are required at least one piece is to be selected from the thickest batch from each 'cast'.

When the surveyor is satisfied in all respects, every plate and section is required to be clearly stamped with the Society's brand ℞ and, in addition, with marks to enable the grade of steel, the steelworks, and the heat from which the piece was made, to be identified.

LLOYD'S REGISTER TESTS FOR STEEL CASTINGS

Tensile tests to be made after heat treatment; tensile 26–35 tons/in² elongation 20 per cent minimum on standard test piece.

Cold bend test Test piece to bend through an angle of 120 degrees without fracture.

As the sizes of test pieces influence the results as recorded by testing machines the Classification Societies agreed to adopt a standard gauge length.

Rivet tests Steel rivets are almost invariably used in ship construction, where high-tensile steel is employed, rivets of the same quality are used.

Bend test Sample rivets to be capable of being bent cold, and being hammered until the sides of the shank touch, without showing signs of fracture at the outside of the bend.

Forge test The head to be flattened when hot until the diameter is $2\frac{1}{2}$ times the diameter of the rivet without cracking at the edges.

Aluminium

Aluminium in the pure state is rarely used in ships due to its low mechanical strength since the minimum tensile strength is from 4 to 9 tons/in² according to purity. The strength however can be increased by alloying with other metals and these aluminium alloys are being increasingly used for superstructures, deckhouses, casings, funnels and for the construction of lifeboats. The weight of aluminium is about one-third that of steel and while the scantlings may require to be increased due to the lower tensile strength, the saving in weight may be such as to justify the use of the aluminium alloy in spite of its relatively high cost.

Welding

The modern method of welding is an extension of the principle of soldering by fusing the edges of the material to be joined. Of the processes available electric arc welding is the most important and covered electrodes—the burning points of the welding tools—are mass-produced for manual and automatic welding. The shipbuilding industry, the largest consumer of steel material, has developed the welding technique and it is the major method employed of making structural connections. The welding of ship's plates under the livid flame of the electrode arc was a major revolution in the technique of ship construction. The first ship to be fully welded was the 150-ft vessel *Fullager*, built by Cammell Laird of Birkenhead and classed in Lloyd's Register Book for 1920. Welding has many advantages both economic and technical. The weight of steel used is less and some parts have been eliminated. Overlapped plates and connecting flanges on structural sections are no longer necessary; stiffening angles can be toe welded.

Figure 28 shows the various types of welds in general use.

(1) *Butt Weld*   In this type of weld the plate edges can be prepared as shown. Generally for plates above $\frac{3}{4}$ in thick it is necessary to 'V' the plate from both edges. (1a) Where hand welding is employed an included angle of 50–60 degrees is generally necessary. Where a machine weld is adopted the angle can be considerably less.

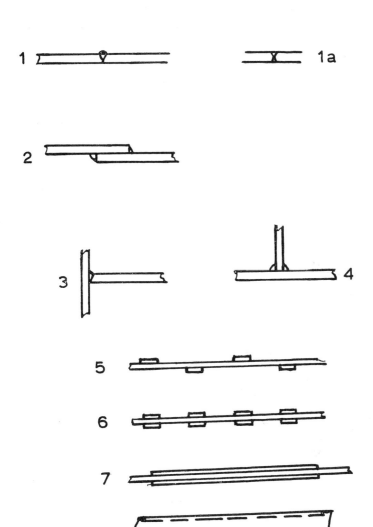

28 Types of welds

(2) *Lap Weld*   This is made by two fillet welds. In main strength members the butt weld is superior.

(3) This is a T connection made by preparing the edge of one plate. The weld is similar to a butt weld.

(4) This is also a T connection made by two fillet welds. If the connection is to be watertight or oiltight the fillet welds should be continuous.

Where a stiffener is to be connected to plating it is generally done by one of the following methods:

(5) Staggered intermittent welding. These are fillet welds made on alternate sides of the stiffener; each weld has a length of about 3 in and the distance between centres on alternate sides may vary between 5 in and 8 in. This could replace a single riveted connection.

(6) Chain intermittent welding. This is as staggered intermittent welding but gives twice the amount of welding. This could replace a double-riveted connection.

(7) Continuous welding. A continuous fillet weld is deposited on each side of the member.

(8) Scalloped welding: this involves taking a scallop out of the web of the stiffener, the scallop is generally 6 in long with a depth one-quarter of the stiffener depth with a maximum of 3 in.

Hand welding is employed for awkward corners and generally for overhead, but welding is easiest and more efficient where it can be made downhand. Hence as much welding as possible is carried out under cover in welding shops on flat panels by automatic welding. It is common practice to adopt prefabricated welded panels. The size of these is controlled by the lifting facilities of the shipyard. Welding machines are in general use, not only for butt welds but also for fillet welding. Some shipyards have welding gantries in the prefabrication sheds. These span the shed, enabling the welding equipment to be positioned rapidly and with ease. This eliminates constant crane attendance.

Riveting

Rivets are still employed, to a limited extent, as means of connecting parts of a ship's structure. The use of rivets has a number of disadvantages; the weight involved in the form of edge and buttlaps, butt straps, angle flanges, etc., which are required solely for the purpose of riveting is quite extensive and indeed amounts in the aggregate to an appreciable proportion of that required for strength.

It is obvious that the ship structure will be unsatisfactory unless the various parts of the hull are efficiently connected. Consequently good workmanship in riveting is of vital importance. Rivet holes, punched or drilled, are slightly greater in diameter than the rivet, so as to allow the entry of the rivet in the heated state. When the rivet is properly clenched the hole should be completely filled.

There are several forms of rivets, but the panhead is more or less the standard form of rivet used in shipbuilding. It is of conical form just under the head and for watertight or oiltight work the panhead rivet with conical neck and countersunk point is very suitable (Figure 29). In addition to the watertightness of the

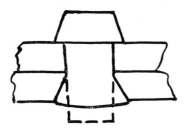

29 Standard form of rivet

countersunk point there is the advantage of an almost flush surface which is essential for positions such as shell plating, decks and the inner bottom plating. The soundness of individual rivets may be tested by tapping the head or point with a small hammer. Loose, cracked or broken rivets can generally be detected by the sound.

E

Caulking

Riveted joints cannot be relied upon to be completely watertight or oiltight under pressure without undergoing the process of being caulked. In overlap joints a chisel-like tool with a bevelled face, known as a 'splitter', is held closely against and splits the upstanding edge. Another tool is then used to force the partly detached material against the surface of the adjacent plate. Caulking is tested by trying to insert a thin steel blade or 'feeler' into the joint.

Corrosion

Corrosion or rusting is an oxidation of the steel. Wasting of steel in the presence of sea water may be uniform or concentrated and when confined to small points, creating indentations, is known as 'pitting'. Considerable expenditure on the upkeep of ships is brought about by repairs necessitated by wastage. The protection of the structure against wastage, apart from wear and tear, is thus of very great importance to shipowners and to those concerned with the maintenance of ships. The oxidation of steel in ships is principally caused by chemical action but may also arise from other causes such as electrolytic action. When steel is exposed to the atmosphere or water, corrosion is promoted by the presence of carbonic-acid gas. Due to the salts in sea water, corrosion is more active in sea water than in fresh.

Effective corrosion prevention or control commences with clean material. Steel material as delivered to the shipyard contains mill scale and rust. This formation of scale on mild steel in the process of manufacture is another form of oxidation. If part of the scale is dislodged, as happens in the working of the material in the shipyard, the remaining scale sets up electrolytic action and corrosion becomes intense on the uncovered parts. Mill scale can be successfully removed by 'shot-blasting'. This is a method of descaling and consists of projecting an abrasive against the steel plates or sections at a high velocity. Plants are available for treating both plates and bars in the same equipment or separately. To obtain the maximum benefit from the shot-blasting process the steel surfaces should be given a shop paint primer as soon as possible after blasting. It has been suggested that the delay permissible between the processes is about 20 minutes or less, depending upon humidity. Special primers are available which dry rapidly and permit almost immediate handling of the steel.

The economic life of a tanker depends on a variety of factors and an important one is corrosion. The corrosion of the structure in oil tanks is related to the service and in general motor spirit is much more actively corrosive than the heavier kinds of oil. There is always a certain amount of water left after steaming out and washing down the tanks and this sets up corrosion particularly at the bottom.

Lloyd's rules now provide that where an approved system of corrosion control is fitted the thickness of certain parts of the structure may be reduced by 10 per cent. The approved system of corrosion control may be either a protective coating or the adoption of cathodic protection.

There is a type of paint based on epoxy resin, which is being used by most large tanker owners. It gives an enamel finish reputed to be impervious to steam, oil, water, etc., and to have lasting qualities. Epoxy coatings require a high standard of preparation and application. Selective painting of cargo tanks together with cathodic protection is in many cases being used to preserve the steelwork. Cathodic protection is the polarisation. of the metallic structure by the introduction of a second metal which acts as an anode. The efficiency of cathodic protection depends on adequate ballasting and the maintenance of the hull potential within the required limits.

To maintain all parts of the structure in an efficient condition it is essential that they should be subject to periodical inspection and for that purpose they must be easily accessible. In very narrow spaces at the extreme ends of the ship, where access for repainting is difficult if not impossible, it is advisable to fill such places solid with cement or other air-excluding substance. Experience has clearly shown that in confined spaces, where foul air may accumulate, condensation of moisture takes place and consequently corrosion is rapid. Provision should therefore be made for ample ventilation to all storerooms and similar compartments. Maintenance costs can be reduced by attention to accessibility, adequate drainage and clean structural design.

Painting

The primary object of painting steelwork is to provide a coating that will protect the surface from the oxidising effect of the air or water. The first, or priming, coat is the most important, as to be effective it must adhere closely to the surface, be airtight and watertight and completely cover the surface. In ship work the first coat is commonly a paint with red lead as the basic pigment and boiled linseed oil; this among other things has the advantage that it will dry comparatively quickly and assist the succeeding coat to set.

Paint and painting absorb a considerable proportion of maintenance costs. Effectiveness in arresting corrosion and durability depends not only upon the quality of the paint but also to a large extent on the thoroughness of surface preparation, weather conditions prevailing and the techniques used during application.

Fouling

What is known as fouling is the growth and accumulation of vegetable and animal life on the immersed hull of ships. The rate of fouling depends on local conditions and on temperature and is far from being uniform in the same district. A fair average for one year in temperate waters without docking appears to be an increase in surface friction of 100 per cent. This implies a daily average rate of 0·27 per cent. Fresh water kills off many sea-water growths, so that the most favourable conditions for ocean-going ships are when the terminal ports are in fresh water.

The roots of many marine growths and the attachments of many forms of marine life, when they get a hold, penetrate the paint, adhere to the plating and as a result set up corrosion and pitting. In the past a number of systems of protection have been tried, but the application of anti-fouling paints and fairly frequent cleaning in dry dock are the methods now usually adopted. The efficacy of anti-fouling paints depends upon their ability to prevent adherence of marine life and to poison marine growths. Such paints usually have a toxic content destructive to low forms of marine life and growths, but the effect is limited and generally the composition needs renewal after nine or twelve months. Anti-fouling paints are not generally also anti-corrosive, so that they should be applied only after the surface has been well treated by a coat of anti-corrosive paint. The aim is to produce a hull which will require no maintenance between dockings and which will resist the fouling and roughening that causes deterioration in hull performance.

Bituminous coatings

Bituminous mixtures are frequently preferred to oil paints for certain parts of the ship as anti-corrosive coverings. These bituminous compositions are used, in general, for inside work, tank top plating, bunkers, etc., and when properly applied make most efficient coatings.

Cement

At one time cement was used in single-bottom ships, being spread from bilge to bilge to form a good protection for the bottom plating against the action of bilge water. Cement was also used quite extensively on the bottom plating within the range of the double bottom tank. Today the insides of the shell plating in double-bottom tanks are very often treated with a bituminous composition. Epoxy paints have been developed which give effective protection to the steelwork in single- and double-bottom ships and are accepted by Lloyd's for places where formerly cement was required.

Cement wash

Cement mixed with water to the consistency of paint is often applied to the interior of fresh-water tanks after the surfaces have been painted. This cement wash offers little in the way of pro-tection against corrosion due to the thinness of layer, but if renewed at intervals it keeps the surfaces sweet and clean, and acts as a deodoriser.

Annual and docking surveys

All steel ships classed by Lloyd's Register are subject to survey at intervals of approximately one year. Ships should also be examined in dry dock at intervals of about 12 months.

Special surveys

All steel ships classed by Lloyd's are also subject to Special Surveys every fourth year, but it is possible to obtain a one-year deferment subject to ship being found in satisfactory condition at a special examination held at the end of the fourth year. The details of these surveys are stated in the Rules.

Double bottoms

Double bottoms are almost universal except in small ships. The double bottom creates a structure which can withstand a considerable amount of damage to the outer shell by grounding without flooding the holds or machinery spaces, so long as the inner bottom remains intact. A very important advantage lies in the provision of spaces for the carriage of oil fuel, fresh and feed water and water ballast. The International Convention on Safety of Life at Sea requires that every passenger ship over 330 ft in length, and to which the Convention applies, be fitted with a double bottom extending from the fore-peak bulkhead to the after-peak bulkhead in so far as this is practicable. The thickness of the inner bottom plating is important because of the paramount duty of this plating as forming part of the bottom flange of the 'hull girder'. In moderate-sized ships it is customary to have only the centreline longitudinal girder as a division between tanks, thus making the tanks in pairs, one port and one starboard.

A duct keel forming a centreline pipe tunnel within the double bottom is frequently fitted to provide a convenient place to run fore-and-aft piping. Such an arrangement ensures that the pipes can be under observation at all times.

Access to double-bottom tanks is provided by means of man-holes cut in the inner bottom plating. These are closed by elliptical plates bedded down over studs or the plates are sometimes dished and secured by strong backs.

Air pipes

These are fitted to double-bottom tanks at the opposite end to that at which the filling pipes are placed or at the highest part of the tank. They are used for the relief of air from the tanks when being filled and are led to the open. The height above the freeboard or superstructure deck is governed by the load-line regulations. Satisfactory means permanently attached must be provided for closing the openings of the air pipes in bad weather.

Sounding pipes

These are for the purpose of ascertaining the depth of liquid in the tanks and extend to the bulkhead deck. Sounding pipes should, when possible, be straight, but where this is not practicable the curvature of the pipes must permit the ready passage of the sounding rod or chain. It is important that a doubling plate be fitted below the sounding pipe to protect the plating or alternatively the ends of the pipe can be perforated with small holes to admit the liquid.

Testing

All double-bottom tanks both prior to launching and at subsequent special surveys have to undergo pressure tests. The compartments are filled with water and then pressed up to the greatest head likely to be experienced in practice. The following example illustrates the method of assessing the extent of the pressures involved.

EXAMPLE

A double-bottom tank is 65 ft long and 34 ft wide. It is filled with water to a height of 35 ft in the air pipe above the tank top. Determine (a) the intensity of pressure on the tank top (b) total pressure on the tank top. Assume the water weighs 64 lb per cu ft.

The pressure (P) is given by the expression P=HAW
where P=total load in lb.
H=depth of centroid of area from surface of fluid in ft.
A=immersed area of surface in sq ft.
W=weight of a cubic foot of the liquid in lb.
thus (a) Intensity of pressure on tank top per sq ft=35 × 1 × 64.

$$=2240 \text{ lb}$$

(b) total pressure on tank top=pressure per sq ft × area of tank top.

$$=\frac{2240 \times 65 \times 34}{2240} = 2210 \text{ tons}$$

Shell plating

The shell plating of a ship has two independent functions to fulfil. Its primary function is to act as a watertight envelope and enable the vessel to displace water. It is also the principal longitudinal strength member of the 'hull girder'. The shell plating is arranged in a series of fore and aft 'strakes' and the strake of the side plating running fore and aft at the deck is known as the sheerstrake.

The thickness of the shell plating amidships is governed by considerations of longitudinal strength and must be adequate to resist shear. The thickness does not usually vary in the girth of the ship other than that the keel plate is thicker than the rest of the bottom plating and the sheerstrake is generally thicker than the rest of the side plating. The thickness is, however, reduced gradually from amidships to the ends of the ship. The following requirements are laid down by Lloyd's Register. (a) The region of the bottom shell to be strengthened to resist pounding is between 0·05L and 0·25L from the fore end. (b) The regions to have special strengthening to resist panting are the after peak tank and the portion forward of 0·15L from the fore end.

Where there are openings in the shell plating, or a sudden discontinuity of strength or break in the erections, the shell plating is increased in thickness.

Figure 30a shows a form of rounded gunwale which is now quite common in the construction of tankers and dry cargo ships.

This method is superior to that of (b), as it eliminates the source from which a notch-brittle fracture might emanate. A minimum radius of 15 times the plate thickness is required in this construction.

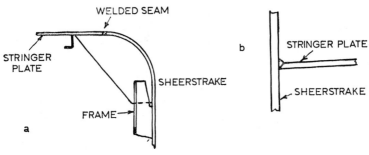

30 Rounded gunwale

Side framing

The side frames of a ship have two main functions. (a) They act as stiffeners holding the side-shell plating against external water pressure. (b) They provide, when transverse, vertical support to the outboard ends of the beams supporting the various decks. Side framing may be transverse or longitudinal. If the longitudinals are made effectively continuous through transverse bulkheads they contribute quite appreciably to the section modulas of the hull girder and hence assist in resisting the longitudinal bending of the ship's hull. However, the deep transverses required to support the longitudinal framing in both holds and tween decks have serious disadvantages; in dry cargo ships they interfere with cargo stowage.

It appears that an upper deck and double bottom framed longitudinally in association with transverse framing on the side shell is the most successful combination for modern cargo ships.

Decks

Steel decks serve three purposes: (1) They form platforms to carry cargo and other loads. (2) They contribute to longitudinal strength and (3) the weather deck forms the top of the watertight envelope which keeps water out of the ship. The plating is usually worked in strakes arranged longitudinally; the strakes which are adjacent to the ship's sides are termed 'stringer plates' and are of considerable importance as they form the connection between the deck and shell plating. They are, thus, generally of greater thickness than the remainder of the deck plating. Figure 31 shows

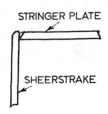

31 Connection of sheerstrake and stringer

one form of connection. The large openings in decks for cargo hatches, machinery casings, etc., are potential sources of weakness and consequently additional transverse and longitudinal strength has to be incorporated in the structure to compensate for the loss of continuity in the deck plating. The deck plating may be supported by transverse beams or longitudinals; see also note under side framing. If cargo is suspended from a deck, as in the case of meat hanging from the deck overhead, then additional strengthening must be introduced in order to carry the suspended load in addition to the normal load on the deck.

Deck plating between and within the outboard edge of large openings, such as cargo hatchways and machinery casings, is usually lighter than the continuous plating outboard of the openings; this gives an efficient distribution of material.

Bulkheads

Bulkheads in ships serve one or more of the following functions: (a) provide structural support to the hull, (b) divide the ship into watertight compartments so that in the event of damage admitting water to the vessel this water will be confined to the damaged region, (c) act as divisional partitions and thus form the boundaries of water or fuel tanks.

The classification rules require that cargo ships of ordinary design be fitted with transverse watertight bulkheads of a number depending on the ship's length and the position of the machinery space. Lloyd's Rules for watertight bulkheads are as follows:

(1) A collision bulkhead must be fitted at a distance not less than 5 per cent and not more than $7\frac{1}{2}$ per cent of the vessel's length from the fore part of the stem at the waterline.

(2) An after-peak bulkhead to be fitted and so arranged as to enclose the shaft tubes in a watertight compartment.

(3) A bulkhead to be fitted at each end of the machinery space. Then additional bulkheads are to be fitted, the number depending on the length of the ship. Transverse bulkheads should extend to the bulkhead deck. The collision bulkhead has to extend to the uppermost continuous deck.

The usual structural arrangements for bulkheads consists of horizontal strakes of plating supported by a system of vertical stiffeners. The thickness of the plating is regulated by the distance of the horizontal strakes of plating below the bulkhead deck and according to the spacing of the vertical stiffeners. The scantlings of the stiffeners at the standard spacing of 30 in depend upon the position of the stiffeners relative to the bulkhead deck, their unsupported length of span, and the means of connection at their ends. A bulkhead stiffener may be regarded as a beam or girder having a given span and supporting a distributed load. The effectiveness of the stiffener depends to a large extent upon the nature of the end connections. A higher standard of strength is required in the collision bulkhead due to the greater likelihood of the fore peak being flooded and the bulkhead being thus subjected to impulsive forces. The stiffeners of the collision bulkhead are spaced 24 in apart instead of the normal 30 in spacing.

Water pressure increases in direct proportion to the depth or head so that the mean pressure will be at half-depth and at the water surface the pressure will be nil. The total load on an area such as a bulkhead is given by:

Total load = average pressure per sq ft × area in sq ft. The average pressure per sq ft is the head at the centroid or centre of the area multiplied by the weight of a cubic foot of the liquid involved. The weight of a cubic foot of fresh water is 62·5 lb and for sea water is 64 lb. Thus, as previously given in the section on double bottoms.

P=HAW where P=total load in lb.
H=depth of centre of area from surface of fluid in ft.
A=immersed area of bulkhead in sq ft.
W=weight of a cubic foot of the liquid in lb.

Centre of pressure

This is the point at which the entire pressure on an immersed area can be considered as acting. It is not the centroid or centre of the immersed area but the centre of the pressure or load diagram.

The position of the centre of pressure on a bulkhead will vary with the shape of the bulkhead. In the case of a rectangular bulkhead with the fluid at the top edge the centre of pressure is at two-thirds the depth from the top or one-third the depth from the bottom.

EXAMPLE

To illustrate the principles employed assume a rectangular bulkhead 20 ft wide and with a depth of 25 ft loaded on one side to the top edge with sea water.

From $P=HAW$ Centre of pressure $=25 \times \frac{2}{3}$
$\qquad =25/2 \times 20 \times 25 \times 64/$ $=16\frac{2}{3}$ ft from
$\qquad\qquad 2240$ top of bulkhead
$\qquad =178\cdot5$ tons   or $25/3=8\frac{1}{3}$ ft from
$\qquad\qquad\qquad\qquad\qquad\qquad\qquad$ bottom

This can be shown in graphic form as indicated in Figure 32.
Pressure at top of bulkhead $=0$
Do. bottom Do. $=25 \times 1 \times 64/2240=5/7$ ton/ft^2.
Total water pressure $=$ area of load diagram which in the case of a rectangle is a triangular figure.

$=\frac{1}{2} \times 5/7 \times 25 \times 20$ NOTE: 20 ft is width of bulkhead.
$=178 \cdot 5$ tons as before.

The centroid of the load diagram is the position of the centre of pressure. The centroid of a triangle is one-third of its depth from the base. The centre of pressure is not only the point at which the total pressure of water will be concentrated but is also where the bending moment is at its maximum.

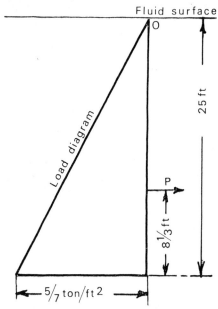

32 Bulkhead loading

Water-pressure tests

Fore-and-aft peak tanks are tested by the peaks being filled with water to a height not less than the load waterline.

Deep tanks and fuel bunkers are tested by filling the spaces with water up to the desired head.

Watertight bulkheads are subjected to a hose test. The pressure of water in the hose should not be less than 30 lb per sq in.

Watertight subdivision of passenger ships

The subdivision of passenger ships by watertight bulkheads is subject to the requirements of the International Convention on Safety of Life at Sea. Details of this convention are given in Chapter IX.

Passenger ships are defined in the Merchant Shipping Acts as those carrying more than 12 passengers.

Hatchways

A hatchway is a large opening cut in the deck to provide access to the hold spaces. In general, hatchways should be as large as feasible, to minimise the amount of horizontal movement required to stow the cargo. There are many factors that affect the final determination of hatch size and position. The first consideration is that of the type of cargo to be carried. If a restrictive cargo is likely, such as heavy machinery, locomotives, long structural steel, etc., then the minimum size is dictated by the requirements for dealing with such a commodity. Limiting conditions obtain, however, as the large openings cut in the deck plating, especially of the strength deck, reduce the effective sectional area of that very important strength member.

It is necessary to protect all weather deck openings against the risk of swamping. Hatchways are framed by the hatch coamings fitted along the sides and ends of the openings and the height of these is important.

Regulations about hatchways are given in the International Convention on Load Lines of 1966 and the following are extracts:

For the purpose of the Regulations, two positions of hatchways are defined:

Position 1

Upon exposed freeboard and raised quarter-decks and upon exposed superstructure decks situated forward of a point located $\frac{1}{4}L$ from the forward perpendicular.

Position 2

Upon exposed superstructure decks situated abaft $\frac{1}{4}L$ from the forward perpendicular.

Hatchways closed by portable covers and secured weathertight by tarpaulins and battening devices:

(a) The coaming of hatchways closed by portable covers secured weathertight by tarpaulins and battening devices shall be of substantial construction and the height above deck shall be at least as follows:

$23\frac{1}{2}$ in if in position 1

$17\frac{1}{2}$ in if in position 2

(b) Where covers are made of wood, the finished thickness shall be at least $2\frac{3}{8}$ in in association with a span of not more than 4·9 ft.

(c) Where covers are made of mild steel the strength has to be calculated with assumed loads the details of which are given in the Regulations.

(d) Cleats shall be set to fit the taper of the wedges. They must be at least $2\frac{1}{2}$ in wide, and spaced not more than $23\frac{1}{2}$ in centre to centre.

(e) Battens and wedges to be efficient and in good condition. Wedges to be of tough wood and have a taper of not more than 1 in 6 and not less than $\frac{1}{2}$ in thick at the toes.

(f) At least two layers of tarpaulins in good condition to be provided for each hatchway in position 1 or 2.

(g) For all hatchways in positions 1 or 2 steel bars to be provided to efficiently secure each section of hatchway covers after the tarpaulins are battened down.

Hatchways closed by weathertight covers of steel or other equivalent material fitted with gaskets and clamping devices.

(a) At positions 1 and 2 the height above the deck of hatchway coamings to be as specified above.

The height of the coamings may be reduced or omitted entirely on condition that the Administration is satisfied that the safety of the ship is not thereby impaired in any sea conditions. Where coamings are provided they shall be of substantial construction.

(b) Where weathertight covers are of mild steel the strength has to be calculated with assumed loads the details of which are given in the Regulations.

(c) The means of securing and maintaining weathertightness shall ensure that the tightness can be maintained in any sea conditions and for this purpose tests are required at least at the initial survey.

Figure 33 shows a steel hatch folding cover, which can have electric or hydraulic actuation and is by Cargo-Dynamics (GB) Ltd.

Building new ships afloat

A new and striking departure from normal shipbuilding practice has been carried out successfully in Japan. The system known as

33 Steel hatch folding cover

the 'at-sea hull connecting technique' was tested by Mitsubiski Heavy Industries at the Yokohama Yard in the presence of government officials and classification society representatives. The tests were conducted using a 40,000-ton deadweight tanker. The fore-and-aft bodies of the tanker, which were cut earlier and provided with watertight 'jackets', were successfully connected while moored at a pier instead of in a dock. Such a system could obviate the need for the construction of new building facilities for the very large vessels at present under consideration.

To build additional facilities to meet the increasing demand for larger ships would require heavy capital outlay. By using the at-sea connecting technique the capital outlay would be relatively small as the forward and after bodies could be built separately on existing berths, modified for the purpose, and then connected at a pier.

III · NOTES ON MARINE MACHINERY
AND AUXILIARIES

Marine propulsion machinery can be classified broadly under two headings—steam and internal combustion.

The reciprocating steam engine

A steam engine is one which receives its power from an external source in the form of steam, generated from water in a boiler by the application of heat.

It consists of one or more cylinders, each containing a piston which moves up and down within the cylinders and attached to a piston rod which is associated with a connecting rod and crank secured to the crankshaft.

The reciprocating steam engine is in fact the oldest form of marine power transmission and has existed in one form or another for over 150 years. It depends for its operation on the expansive working of the steam; if steam is supplied under pressure to a closed cylinder and allowed to expand it will push the piston along the cylinder. However, one expansion is not enough as the steam when it leaves the high-pressure cylinder still possesses energy. Consequently it is expanded until most of the energy has been extracted, sometimes twice and sometimes three times, in cylinders of increasing diameter. The engine is known under these conditions respectively as a triple or quadruple expansion engine.

After leaving the last stage of expansion of the engine it goes to the condenser where the steam in tubes, coming into contact with cold sea water, is condensed to water again and eventually pumped back into the boiler. Thus there is closed circulation except for losses by leakage, condensation, etc., and the full amount of water in the system is kept constant by make-up feed arrangements.

The first passenger steamship in Europe was Henry Bell's paddle steamer *Comet*, which commenced passenger service on the Clyde between Glasgow and Greenock in August 1812. This vessel was powered by an engine with a single vertical cylinder $12\frac{1}{2}$ in diameter and 16 in stroke. Steam was supplied by a low-pressure land boiler.

Due to lack of financial success the *Comet* had to be withdrawn from service, but the fact that such a service was a practical proposition had been demonstrated and marine steam propulsion was thereby established in Britain. By 1822 there were some 140 steam vessels in this country and in 1825 there were 51 steamships in service on the Clyde.

The steam turbine

This is a rotary machine and consists of a number of blades attached to a rotor fixed to the shaft. Enclosed in a cylinder are also fixed guiding blades. As the steam is admitted into the cylinder at high velocity it impinges and expands on both the fixed blades of the cylinder and the moving blades on the rotor, giving a rotary motion to the shaft. As the steam passes over the blades it loses pressure and increases in expansion.

In a marine steam turbine installation the turbines are grouped round a large gear wheel into which the pinions of each turbine mesh. The main wheel is directly coupled to the propeller line shafting. By means of gearing a high-speed turbine can be arranged to drive a propeller at low speeds. The reduction of the gearing may be either single or double. As the turbines are uni-directional, it is necessary to provide a separate astern turbine.

The steam turbine dates back to 1884 when Charles A. Parsons obtained a patent for a reaction turbine. By 1892 the steam turbine for marine propulsion had become a practical proposition. An experimental boat, the *Turbinia*, was built and ultimately in 1897 attained a speed of 34½ knots.

With steam machinery a steam-raising plant is involved and this consists of cylindrical Scotch boilers or water-tube boilers. Where steam reciprocating machinery is still used, the boilers, generally oil-fired, may be either of the types mentioned. With steam turbines, water-tube boilers must be used to provide the higher temperatures and pressures necessary for this type of machinery.

Boilers

As stated above, there are, broadly, two kinds of boilers, fire-tube or Scotch boiler and water-tube. The Scotch boiler has a series of furnaces connected with a common combustion chamber at the back of the boiler; to this combustion chamber are linked a series of tubes in which the gases generated in the furnace are passed. The gases passing through these tubes give out their heat to the surrounding water.

The Scotch boiler is much more suited to the ordinary cargo steamship than the water-tube boiler. It is cheaper in initial cost, requires less care in maintenance and is capable of using ordinary water without treatment. The boilers are usually now oil-fired.

In the water-tube boiler there is a series of circular tubes connected with 'drums' in which the water is contained. The heat is outside the tube. Water-tube boilers are rapid in steam raising, flexible in output and compact in space for the steam they develop.

The internal combustion engine

This is one which obtains its power from the combustion of fuel inside the cylinder of the engine.

The oil engine, or motor, or diesel engine, or internal combustion engine, or more correctly called the compression ignition engine, is something which has developed enormously since the invention of it by the German, Dr Diesel. Today there are a number of makes built under licence in different parts of the world. The main kinds of diesel engines are referred to as two-cycle, four-cycle and opposed-piston, according to the principle of operation. The oil engine is really an explosion engine. A spray of oil is injected into the space between the top of the cylinder and the bottom of the cylinder cover. Contained in this space is air under compression. When air is under compression it gets hot; at the point of maximum compression, and consequently maximum heat, the fuel valve opens and a small spray of oil is injected; this oil burns rapidly, explodes and drives the piston down in the cylinder. This explosive energy is translated by piston rod, crosshead and connecting rod to the crankshaft which is thereby rotated.

An engine working on the two-cycle principle has one working stroke in every revolution of the crank and completes the working cycle in two strokes. An engine on the four-cycle principle has one working impulse in every two revolutions of the crank or four strokes of the piston in which it completes the cycle of operations.

Gas turbines

At one time there were great expectations from the gas-turbine type of prime mover for ships. A prototype gas-turbine unit was installed in the tanker *Auris* in the early 1950s; this unit did not entirely replace the ship's existing engine and although it was reported as giving a good performance, plans by the owners for a tanker having only a gas-turbine propelling unit did not reach maturity. A major problem is that of burning low-grade boiler fuel in this type of machinery and until this can be solved the gas-turbine is not likely to have a future as an economic means of merchant-ship powering. The attraction of marine gas turbines for naval use is not in question.

Nuclear power

A commercially competitive nuclear power plant for merchant ships is not yet available. The United States of America have the cargo liner *Savannah*, which has been given extensive publicity, and the USSR has the ice-breaker *Lenin*, but neither of these make any claim to economic operation.

Other nations have or expect to have nuclear-powered merchant ships. The British Board of Trade have under consideration a number of commercial-type reactor designs, but such projects are restricted by the factor that any marine nuclear reactor must be economically acceptable or at least have definite prospects of being in this category.

There is no doubt that nuclear power will be used in merchant ships, but many problems must be solved before this is realised. One of the major problems is safety. Any attempt to introduce nuclear power for ship propulsion at present is made more difficult by the very high standard of safety required. The solutions to some of the problems are complex and expensive. Many reactors can be built and operated safely, although their evolution as useful and economic systems must inevitably await the accumulation of experience through research and prototype tests.

Automation

The day of the fully automated ship has not yet arrived. However, ships which have centralised and remote control, rather than outright automatic control, are very much on the increase. The grouping of engine controls and instrumentation in soundproofed glassed-in and air-conditioned control rooms located in the ship's engine room is the main feature of centralised control. In this way watch-keeping is simplified and overall visual observation of the installation still possible. Remote control relates, in general, to systems of direct control of the ship's propelling power from the navigating bridge. This type of control has been in operation for some years in diesel-powered ferries, trawlers, coasters, etc.

In general there has been more development of automatic control in diesel-engined ships than in vessels with steam-turbine machinery. In the marine steam installation the main hindrance to fully automatic control lies in the oil-fuel burners, although much is being done to overcome this difficulty.

The Classification Societies are very interested and active in this matter and guidance notes under the heading 'Automation in Ships' were issued by Lloyd's Register in 1963. Bureau Veritas also issued, in 1963, guidance notes under the heading, 'General Technical Conditions Concerning the Automation of Ships'.

The advantages of automation are a reduction in personnel, greater fuel economy, better control of machinery, etc. On the other side there are factors as cost of automation equipment, increased maintenance, etc. Automation is definitely on its way and may well prove to be the most significant development in present-day marine engineering.

Auxiliaries

The engine room of a ship has two main aspects; that concerned with the propulsion of the ship and that concerned with the supply of power. Thus power is required (a) for the operation of the propelling unit and (b) for the running of the ship. The main engine and boilers, when the latter are installed, require pumps; the ship requires pumps for domestic and sanitary purposes; power is also required for heating, lighting and cooking. In addition power is necessary for (a) steering the ship, (b) for the winches when the ship is in port handling cargo, and (c) for the windlass when the vessel is coming to port, anchoring.

All this auxiliary equipment is entirely separate from the main propelling machinery.

Electricity was for many years used on board ship exclusively for lighting purposes. Its introduction for the myriad purposes for which it is now employed was undertaken slowly, but once initial difficulties were overcome its use grew very rapidly. In the engine room today electricity is used for auxiliary purposes on two sides: the domestic side and the ship side. In the machinery space practically all the pumps associated with the main propelling unit, be it steam or diesel, are electrically operated. This is, in the main, because on the whole they are compact, clean in operation, smooth-running, easy to overhaul and, most important, easy to control.

The make-up of a typical cargo ship's electrical service is given below:

SEA LOAD

Engine room auxiliaries
Steering gear

Domestic service—light, heat, cooking, ventilation, refrigeration.
Navigational equipment
Cargo refrigeration—if any

HARBOUR LOAD

Cargo handling—winches, cranes
Deck service—windlass, capstan
Domestic service—as in sea load.

Selection of machinery

The selection of the type of propelling machinery to be adopted for merchant ships is based upon its reliability in service and the cost of operation and maintenance.

For the average general cargo ship, steam reciprocating machinery, even with up-to-date refinements, is not today looked upon as being economically acceptable. Steam turbines, due to their relatively high fuel consumption, are also not economically attractive. Hence in the low and medium power ranges the diesel engine with its low fuel consumption has taken over where the steam reciprocating engine has once been supreme. Most motor cargo ships have machinery of the slow-running type directly connected to the propeller shaft. The trend today is to have more power in less space and current practice is to turbocharge existing standard-type diesel engines. For the average general cargo ship the best proposition seems to be a turbocharged, two-stroke direct drive diesel using the exhaust gases for a waste-heat boiler and burning residual fuels.

Steam turbine machinery even in its most advanced stage is unable to compete with the low fuel-consumption rates of the diesel. Generally, however, the total weight of the installation is less that that of the corresponding motor ship and maintenance and repair bills are lower. To make the steam turbine more competitive efforts are being made towards reductions in initial cost and fuel consumption. The major item in a marine steam turbine cost is the reduction gear. This gear is the largest unit and is an important factor in engine room weight and space required for installation. Steam turbines are continually being improved and a re-heat turbine has been installed in one of the world's very large tankers. The steam turbine will likely continue to be used in ships where reliability and freedom from vibration are important factors—passenger ships.

Propulsion analysis

A propulsion analysis of world tonnage shows the changeover from steam to diesel; from 1939 to 1967.

	1967 %	1939 %
Reciprocating engines	10·7	61·1
Turbine engines	30·4	14·2
TOTAL STEAM	41·1	75·3
Diesel engines	58·9	24·7
	100·0	100·0

Fuel analysis

A fuel analysis of world tonnage shows:

	%
Steamships burning coal	2·3
Steamships burning oil	44·5
Motorships	53·2
	100·0

The propeller

The primary part of any marine power plant is the propeller. The paddle wheel is now found only in relatively few cases. Paddle machinery has virtually disappeared from seagoing ships not so much on account of any propulsive inefficiency but because of its vulnerability, greater cost and its unsuitability for large changes in draught.

While the screw propeller had probably been first proposed by Hooke in 1681 and again by Watt in 1784, a screw propeller was actually patented in Great Britain in 1785 by one Joseph Bramah. The screw was finally brought into general use by the efforts of John Ericsson, a Swedish engineer, who took out a patent in 1836. Francis Smith also obtained a patent on a screw propeller in the same year. He carried out successful trials, with a launch fitted with his propeller, on the Paddington Canal in 1837. As a result of these trials a syndicate was formed and the *Archimedes* was built for this company and fitted with a propeller. This ship accomplished the circumnavigation of Great Britain, made a voyage to Oporto and thus established screw propulsion for sea-going ships. This vessel was, in fact, the first seagoing steamer to be fitted with a screw propeller. The first screw-propelled steamer to cross the Atlantic was the *Great Britain* in 1845.

Many theories have been advanced to explain the phenomena of screw propulsion. The first theories considered the motion of the propeller as a nut on a screw, but allowed for slip because of the medium. The theories can be divided into two main groups: those concerned with the momentum changes produced in the fluid and those concerned with the lift and drag forces arising from the motion of a given blade surface. A detailed treatment of these theories is outside the scope of this book.

Pure theory plays a small part in the practical design of propellers; methods of comparison with the results of scale-model experiments have been devised which offer a very good substitute. Nevertheless, theory has often indicated the way to the most profitable lines of experimental research.

A screw propeller has two or more blades projecting from a boss. The surface of each blade when viewed from aft is called the FACE and the other surface is called the BACK.

A propeller is said to be right-handed if when viewed from astern it rotates in the clockwise direction when driving the ship ahead. In ships with twin screws one is right-handed and the other left-handed. Generally the right-handed screw is on the starboard side and thus the propellers are outward turning. The leading edge of a blade is the edge which, when the ship is driven ahead, first cuts the water. The trailing edge is the following edge. The diameter of a propeller is the diameter of the circle swept out by the tips of the blades. The pitch is the distance any specified point on the face of the blade would move forward in one revolution if turning on a solid nut. Pitch ratio is the pitch divided by the diameter. The disc area is the area enclosed within the tip circle. Slip is defined as the difference between the distance which a screw would advance during one revolution if working in a solid medium and the distance it actually advances in a given medium. The pitch of a propeller is one of its most important features as it has a considerable influence on propeller performance.

An important factor affecting propeller efficiency is diameter and in general the larger the better, but the optimum diameter may not be possible due to practical considerations at the stern of the ship. The pitch ratio determines the amount of slip with which the screw will work and for good results this should be in the region of 20 per cent.

The surface area of the propeller blades is another important feature. The shape of the blade outline may vary quite a lot in present-day propellers but in the past the usual outline was elliptical. The blades must be of such a shape that their resistance to motion through the water is small. Two types of blade sections are shown in Figure 34a is the flat-face circular-back type, the thickness reducing to almost zero at the leading and trailing edges and greatest at the centre of the breadth. The back of sections of this type are circular arcs. (b) is the aerofoil type extensively used in modern propellers. The main differences between (a) and (b) are that in (b) the maximum thickness is nearer the leading edge than the centre of the breadth and the leading edge is more rounded. Blade sections become thinner towards the tips, the greatest thickness occurring at the root or the inner end of the blade which is attached to the boss.

Due to incessant demands for higher propulsive efficiency the design and manufacture of propellers has become very complex and the work is carried out by a few specialist engineering companies.

There are three principal types now manufactured—built, solid and controllable pitch propellers—each in general having three, four or five blades.

The 'built' propeller has the blades and hub cast and machined separately and is assembled by bolting each blade to a flange on the hub. The advantage derived from this is that if a blade be damaged it can readily be replaced without removing the entire propeller from the shaft. There is, however, some loss of efficiency with this design and the type is now being replaced by the solid propeller.

a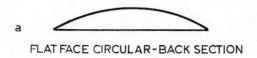

FLAT FACE CIRCULAR-BACK SECTION

b

AEROFOIL SECTION

34 Propeller blade sections

The 'solid' propeller has the blades cast integrally with the hub and today this type is a high efficiency design incorporating streamline blade sections commonly referred to as aerofoil sections.

The 'controllable pitch propeller' is the outcome of development to provide greater flexibility and manœuvrability for certain classes of ships. As the name indicates the pitch can be altered as required to suit prevailing resistance conditions. This is attained by rotating each blade about its axis either by hydraulic or mechanical means. The control gear is inboard and the operating mechanism is located inside the shaft and hub, and the propeller can, in general, be controlled direct from the bridge with the engine running at the normal revolutions. This type of propeller is particularly useful for (a) tugs and trawlers, where the towing and running free conditions are entirely different and (b) ferries and ships with uni-directional prime-movers.

The majority of ocean-going merchant ships have four-bladed screws. A two-bladed screw would require wide blades to provide the thrust required. For many years after their introduction propellers were of simple design and were of cast iron. Modern propellers are of high tensile brass allied with a relatively small content of manganese. This produces a tough and ductile material which facilitates machining. A photograph of a four-bladed propeller is given in Figure 35.

35 Four-bladed propeller, by Stone Manganese Marine Ltd

Cavitation

The phenomenon known as cavitation in marine propellers became evident with the increase in power used which resulted in high thrust per unit area of blade surface. Cavitation was first experienced with high-speed craft in the 1890s and Parsons was confronted with it in his experiments on the *Turbinia*. Cavitation may be briefly described as the formation of cavities round the propeller blade—often on the back of the blade—these cavities being filled with air or water vapour. The effect of cavitation on a propeller is twofold: (a) the cavities formed eventually collapse resulting in a severe mechanical action which produces erosion of the blade surface, (b) if the cavitation is severe a loss in propulsive efficiency is the result. A partial solution to the problem is to increase the blade area of the propeller which means increasing the breadth of the blades. Heavily loaded screws require more blade area than lightly loaded screws.

Two lines of research have been adopted in connection with the problem of cavitation. The first is to study the pressure distribution round the blade sections. Mathematical methods have been devised so that this can be done. The second is an experimental approach. A special type of experiment has been devised where the propeller operates in a closed channel and where the pressure in the fluid can be controlled. This type of channel is known as a cavitation tunnel. Water is circulated through the tunnel: the propeller being tested is stationary in the axial direction but capable of rotation at any desired revolutions. The propeller can be viewed through windows in the tunnel. A pump is used to reduce the static pressure at the propeller and the water speed past the propeller can be measured. As the propeller rotates the thrust and torque can be measured. In order to observe when cavitation is commencing stroboscopic lighting is used which illuminates the propeller giving one flash per revolution. Thus the propeller when viewed through the window appears to be stationary and the formation of cavities round the blades can be observed. In this way model propeller performance can be studied under cavitating conditions.

Figure 36 is a photograph of a propeller taken in a cavitation tunnel.

36 Propeller in cavitation tunnel

Table 1 gives ship and propeller particulars for a cargo vessel and a large tanker.

TABLE I

Type	Dead Weight [tons]	B.H.P.	R.P.M.	Speed [Knots]	Propeller Diameter [ft]	Pitch [ft]	Weight [Tons]
Cargo Ship	13,000	16,600	110	20·5	21·0	19·36	22·77
Tanker	100,000	25,000	105	16	24·5	15·82	34·26

IV · SHIP CLASSIFICATION AND MAINTENANCE

Ships and their cargoes have at all times represented relatively large capital, subject to loss or damage by the perils of the sea. This necessitates the adoption of a system of marine insurance. Marine insurance forms one of the very important divisions in the operations of the shipping industry. Without the assistance given by the underwriter commerce would come to a standstill. The business of insuring ships and their cargoes on their lawful occasions probably started just as soon as men of one nation began trading with those of another across the seas. It is recorded that the Phoenicians, the Venetians and the Hanseatic merchants all had their systems of insurance against the hazards of the sea.

Many of the hazards of the sea can only be guarded against by the skill and courage of the merchant navy officer but a great deal also depends upon the structural fitness of the ship for the service in which it operates. On the face of it, the underwriter called upon to accept a maritime risk and the shippers of a valuable cargo would seek some guarantee of the fitness of the vessel concerned for the voyage in prospect. It is known that, centuries ago, certain particulars of ships were recorded for the guidance of underwriters and shippers, and it is reasonable to assume that these lists of shipping were the basis of a straightforward system of classification that enabled good risks to be distinguished from bad. From such a beginning were created reliable organisations for the inspection and maintenance of character of merchant ships. The best known of such organisations is Lloyd's Register of Shipping. Around the year 1668 a number of underwriters met in the coffee house of Edward Lloyd, situated in Tower Street, London, to transact their business. Resulting from these meetings 'Ships' Lists' were prepared on which were inserted certain symbols giving the underwriters some idea of the character of the vessel they were insuring for the hull or cargo. These records were written by hand and were for the use of underwriters only. They were without authority but that was the common origin of the Corporation of Lloyd's and of Lloyd's Register of Shipping and it was many years before they became separate concerns. The locution 'A1 at Lloyds' simply means that the Corporation of Lloyd's as underwriters are guaranteed a first-class risk as defined by the surveyors of Lloyd's Register of Shipping.

In 1692 the underwriters moved to Lombard Street and there the *Lloyd's List* was first printed in 1727; with the exception of the official *London Gazette* this is the oldest daily paper now published. In 1760 the Register of Shipping was established and became known as the Green Book. This book was supported exclusively by the underwriters. In 1799 a new Register Book was produced by the shipowners and this was known as the Red Book. Classes or characters were assigned to ships after inspection by surveyors employed for that purpose but without the assistance of Rules.

In 1834 an amalgamation took place of the two register books, and Lloyd's Register of Shipping was reconsituted and a definite system of classification was established based on a Book of Rules.

Lloyd's Register Book now appears in four volumes and of these three are mainly of specialist interest. Volumes III and IV are really directories, III listing shipowners throughout the world and IV listing shipbuilding and repairing establishments, dry docks, etc. Volume II is the Appendix to the Register Book proper, giving more technical information than is included in the masterpiece, Vol. I. The Register is a supreme work of reference, used and trusted throughout the world. It contains a list as complete as can be ascertained of all sea-going merchant ships in the

G

world of 100 tons gross and above whether classed by Lloyd's Register or not. The number of ships thus listed exceeds 36,000.

Classification Societies

The principal maritime nations have the following Classification Societies:

Great Britain—Lloyd's Register of Shipping.
United States of America—American Bureau of Shipping
France—Bureau Veritas
Germany—Germanischer Lloyd
Norway—Det Norske Veritas
Italy—Registro Italiano
Russia—Register of Shipping of the USSR
Japan—Nippon Kaiji Kyokai.
Poland—Polish Register of Shipping

The Classification Societies operate throughout the world and publish rules and regulations directly related to the structural efficiency of the ship and the reliability of the propelling machinery. In general they have a long history dating back to the era of wooden ships. Classification is purely voluntary on the part of the shipowner, and the only penalty that can be imposed for non-compliance with the Rules is suspension or cancellation of class.

Classification implies that a ship and the machinery conform to the standards published in the rules of the society. The fundamental purpose of classification is to ensure maintenance of seaworthiness of all classed ships. So far as Lloyd's Register of Shipping is concerned, classification entails approval of constructional plans, testing of materials, construction under survey, and recommendation for class from the surveyors by report to the Committee. Following the acceptance of the report by Lloyd's Committee, the certificate of class is issued and the record made in the Register Book.

Classification symbols

Information relating to the various symbols used by the leading Classification Societies are given below. All the details relating to the characters assigned to ships are not listed but sufficient is included to enable the reader to identify the type of ship, the standard of construction, the service and the name of the Society with which the ship is classed.

Lloyd's Register of Shipping

Founded in 1760. Reconstituted in 1834. United with the Underwriters' Registry for Iron Ships in 1885. Amalgamated with the British Corporation in 1949. Head Office: 71 Fenchurch Street, London EC3.

Steel ships built in accordance with the Society's Rules and Regulations, or with alternative arrangements equivalent thereto, will be assigned a class in the Register Book and will continue to be classed so long as they are found, upon examination at the prescribed annual and other periodical surveys, to be maintained in a fit and efficient condition and in accordance with the Rules.

Classification will be conditional upon compliance with the Society's requirements in respect of both hull and machinery.

100 A1. This class is assigned to seagoing ships built in accordance with the Society's Rules and Regulations for the draught required. The Class 100 A1 is also assigned to ships designed for specific purposes such as 100 A1 oil tanker; 100 A1 ore carrier; 100 A1 tug, etc. Four classes of ice strengthening are detailed in the Rules.

Ice Class 1—strengthening is for ships intended to navigate in extreme ice conditions.

The Figure 1 in the character of classification assigned to a ship indicates that her equipment of anchors, chain cables, and hawsers is in good and efficient condition and in accordance with the Rules.

✠ This symbol indicates that the ship was built under the Society's Special Survey and will be classed thus ✠ 100 A1.

Machinery constructed and installed on board in accordance with the rules and on satisfactory completion of trials is assigned the class notation LMC (Lloyd's Machinery Certificate). New machinery for ships intended for classification is to be constructed under the Society's Special Survey and on completion will have the mark ✠ inserted before the machinery class notation. Thus: ✠LMC.

PERIODICAL SURVEYS

Annual surveys

All steel ships should be surveyed at intervals of approximately one year in accordance with the Rules. These annual surveys should, where practicable, be held concurrently with statutory annual or other load line surveys.

Docking surveys

A ship should be examined in dry dock at intervals of about 12 months; the maximum interval is two years.

Special surveys

All-steel vessels classed with Lloyd's are to be subjected to Special Surveys in accordance with the Rules. These surveys become due at five-yearly intervals, the first five years from the date of build or date of Special Survey for Classification, and thereafter five years from the date of the previous Special Survey.

The date of completion of the Special Survey during construction of ships built under the Society's inspection is normally taken as the date of build.

American Bureau of Shipping: Head Office: 45 Broad Street, New York 4, NY. Incorporated by Act of the Legislature of the State of New York, 1862. United with the Great Lakes Register in 1916. Authorised to assign load lines to vessels registered in the United States and other countries.

Authorised to assign load lines to vessels navigating on the Great Lakes registered in the United States and Canada.

✠ A1. Signifies that the vessel has been built under special survey to the full requirements of the Rules for unrestricted ocean service.

Oil carriers. Vessels built under special survey to the rules for vessels intended to carry oil in bulk and are approved for unrestricted ocean service will have the foregoing symbols followed by the notation 'Oil Carrier'.

Special-purpose vessels. Vessels designed for special purposes and built under survey to scantlings approved for the particular purpose and approved for unrestricted ocean service will have the foregoing symbols, followed by a designation of the trade, such as 'Ferry Service', 'Dredging Service', etc.

Geographical limitations. Vessels built under special survey for limited service will have the foregoing symbols but followed by the appropriate limitation, such as 'Great Lakes Service', 'Short Coastwise Service', etc.

Vessels not built under survey. Vessels not built under special survey but submitted for classification will be subjected to a special Classification Survey. When found satisfactory will have the foregoing symbols but the mark ✠ signifying Special Survey during construction will be omitted.

Equipment symbol. The symbol Ⓔ placed after the symbols of classification, thus: ✠ A1 Ⓔ signifies that the equipment of the vessel is in compliance with the requirements of the Rules.

✠ AMS. Indicates that the machinery and boilers have been built and installed under special survey to the full requirements of the Rules and found satisfactory after trial.

When the machinery and boilers have not been built under special survey, but have been accepted for classification, the Maltese Cross is omitted from the symbols.

The continuance of the classification of any vessel is conditional upon the Rule requirements for periodical and other surveys being carried out. For vessels built under Classification Survey the first Special Periodical Survey becomes due four years after the date of build. Subsequent surveys are due four years after the crediting date of the previous Special Survey.

✠ RMC. Indicates that the refrigerating machinery and insulation has been constructed and installed under special survey.

Bureau Veritas. Founded in 1828. Head Office: 31 rue Henri-Rochefort, Paris 17me. London Office of the British Committee: Turban House, 36–8 Botolph Lane, London EC3.

Steel vessels are classed in two divisions represented by Roman numbers I or II. The division is determined by the scantlings of the vessel. Division I corresponds to scantlings in exact conformity with the provisions of Bureau Veritas Rules and division II to scantlings not in exact conformity with the Rules but acceptable.

A character, which is the Bureau Veritas opinion of a ship, is expressed by a fraction: 3/3 is granted to ships in excellent condition, 5/6 to those whose condition is comparatively less suitable and efficient.

The class mark is completed by a group of two figures; the first one indicates the condition of the wood portions of the hull for steel ships; the second one concerns the condition of rigging, anchors and chains; number 1 means excellent condition, number 2 a comparatively less suitable and efficient state.

✠ Indicates that the ship has undergone special survey for classification, during construction.

When a horizontal line appears beneath the Maltese Cross it shows that the ship has been built under the special survey of another Classification Society.

● Indicates that the ship was not constructed to the requirements of a Classification Society but was later accepted for classification. P.R. These letters indicate that the ship is strengthened for navigation in ice.

A single circle around the division indicates that the vessel will float in calm water with one watertight compartment open to the sea.

Double circles around the division indicate that the vessel will float in calm water with two adjacent compartments open to the sea.

Where the division is enclosed within a figure in the shape of a diamond this indicates that the vessel is a passenger ship and complies with the International Convention for the Safety of Life at Sea.

Ships are granted a conventional letter indicating the kind of navigation or service for which they are considered suitable.

L (ocean going ship), R (roadstead service), S (tugs).

The mark F indicates that the requirements of Chapter 2 of the International Convention for the Safety of Life at Sea (London 1960) have been complied with.

The signs are sometimes completed by marks concerning: Anchors and chains: A & CP.

The special service in which the ship is engaged: 'Bulk Carrier', 'Oil in bulk'; 'Liquefied Petroleum Gas'.

The class is valid during a certain period called the 'term', provided the ship is maintained in good condition. This is ascertained by regular surveys—mostly yearly visits—for which the ship is put in dry dock. Once the term, which is normally four years for seagoing ships, has expired, the class may be renewed after a special (reclassification) survey. An example of symbols and marks is:

$$\overset{19}{\underset{60}{\text{✠}}} \; \overset{}{\underset{60}{\diamondsuit}} \; \text{ꓞ} \quad \overset{3/3 \; L \; 1 \cdot 1}{\text{A \& CP}}$$

This is for an ocean-going passenger ship built under special survey and complying with the 1960 International Convention for subdivision and fire-protection. Excellent condition. Anchors and chains have been tested in presence of Bureau Veritas surveyor.

Det Norske Veritas. Established in 1864. Head Office: Oslo, Norway.

✠ This indicates that the vessel is built under the supervision of Det Norske Veritas.

✠ When a black dot appears above the Maltese Cross it indicates that the vessel is built under the supervision of another Classification Society.

1A1 Steel ships of the strength prescribed in the Society Rules are when duly surveyed assigned the Class 1A1. Periodical survey is four years.

If it is found necessary to shorten the four-year term of survey owing to the general condition and age of a vessel, the vessel is assigned Class 1 A2 with a three-year term of survey.

If the strength of a vessel is not in accordance with the Society Rules the vessel will be assigned the Class 2 A2 for restricted service.

A1 This class is assigned to wood ships of the strength prescribed in the Society Rules. The following letters are applied to the same type of ship but of lower class, viz. A2*, A2 or B1—if necessary for restricted service.

N added to the character indicates trading along the Norwegian coast, in the Baltic Sea, etc.

K added to the character indicates coasting trade along coast where the open stretches of water do not exceed 75 nautical miles. The off-shore distance, however, from vessel to a harbour or safe anchorage must never exceed 45 nautical miles.

I added to the character indicates trading on lakes, rivers, or closed-in fjords.

T This letter applies to vessels built of steel which have been strengthened for carrying ore or similar heavy cargo.

F added to the class of a cargo vessel signifies that additional fire protection installations have been complied with in accordance with the Society Rules.

Is–A, Is–B or Is–C added to the class indicates that the vessel is strengthened for navigation in ice according to Society Rules. Is–A, Is–B and Is–C are approved for the Finnish statutory ice dues Class 1A, Class 1B or Class 1C respectively.

O (for passenger ships engaged on a regular service) indicates running surveys of the hull at the owner's request.

When the character is placed within brackets it indicates that the class is invalid on account of the vessel not having been subjected to the surveys prescribed in the Rules or that repairs recommended were not carried out.

Germanischer Lloyd. Established in 1867. Head Office: 2 Hamburg 36, Neuer Wall 86. Germany.

✠ The Maltese Cross indicates the ship was built under the supervision of the Germanischer Lloyd.

When the Maltese Cross is enclosed within a square it indicates that a buoyancy calculation in damaged condition has been proved.

When a BLACK DOT is placed immediately above the symbol of the Maltese Cross it indicates that the vessel was built under the supervision of another Society.

The Germanischer Lloyd assign the following classes with steel sea-going ships:

100 A4 for four years

90 A3 for three years.

The following letters are added to vessels engaged in a special service:

K Great coasting trade

k Small coasting trade

I Inland or river navigation

E Indicates that the vessel has been strengthened for ice

O Indicates that the character is cancelled since the month and year marked thereunder.

✠MC Indicates that the machinery is classed with and was built under the survey of the Germanischer Lloyd.

Machinery installations which do not comply in all respects with the Rules may be assigned the class notation $\overline{\text{MC}}$.

WOODEN seagoing ships are arranged in two classes and subdivided into two divisions:

A1 and A

B1 and B

The arabic figure after the character of classification means validity of class in years.

Nippon Kaiji Kyokai. Established in 1899. Head Office: Tokyo, Japan.

In 1919, the Society entered into Quadruple Alliance with the British Corporation, the American Bureau and the Registro Italiano for the mutual recognition of the classification and survey of vessels. In 1949 the Alliance terminated.

Since that time the Society has entered into agreement to co-operate on classification survey with the Registro Italiano Navale (1951), American Bureau of Shipping (1952), Germanischer Lloyd (1953) and Register of Shipping of the USSR (1961).

The classification of ships is indicated by the following characters:

NS* for the hull and equipment which have been built under Classification Survey of the Society.

MNS* for the machinery which has been built under Classification Survey of the Society.

NS for the hull and equipment which have undergone Classification Survey after construction.

MNS for the machinery which has undergone Classification Survey after construction.

RMC* for refrigerating installations manufactured under Classification Survey.

RMC for refrigerating installations which have undergone Classification Survey after construction.

Special Surveys are carried out at intervals of four years from the date of completion of the Classification Survey or of the previous Special Survey. In Special Surveys ships are examined in dry dock or on a slipway.

Surveys are carried out between the Classification Survey and Special Survey and between consecutive Special Surveys as follows:

Intermediate Survey: Annual Survey.

Intermediate surveys are at intervals of 12 months for passenger ships or 24 months for other ships.

Annual surveys are carried out at intervals of 12 months for ships other than passenger ships.

Registro Italiano Navale. Head Office: Via XX Settembre 8,

Genova. Classification Society for merchant vessels in Italy, established in 1861 as 'Registro Italiano'.

Classification characteristics

Global reliability, expressed by the numbers 100 and 90 corresponding to the first and second class. The characteristic 100 indicates that the hull and machinery have been found 'good'. The characteristic 90 indicates that the hull or the machinery or both have been found 'sufficient'.

Quality

There are two quality marks: A and As (the second may be also temporarily followed by the notation 'Experimental').
Mark A refers to a ship built according to R.I.NA. Rules or to Rules considered equivalent by the Head Office.
Mark As refers to a ship built according to Rules different from R.I.NA's ones, it being, however, understood that the conditions of the ship are satisfactory as far as the ship's special service is concerned. In this case the mark As has the meaning of 'experimental' quality.

The notation 'experimental' shall be temporarily assigned (in addition to mark As) to the vessels entirely or partially built according to plans of a non-traditional or unusual type and having therefore a character of originality retained satisfactory by the R.I.NA. Head Office, on the basis of the examination of the plans, laboratory tests and trials in service-conditions when the ship has been completed.

The notation 'experimental' implies that the judgement may be confirmed or modified after a period of practical operation from time to time fixed by the R.I.NA. Head Office.

The notation 'experimental' will be deleted after the above mentioned operational period, so that the only mark As will remain.

Efficiency

Expressed with the figures 1 and 2 indicating 'good' and 'sufficient' and separately assigned to the hull and to the machinery.

The characteristic 1 shall be granted to new or first classified ships that correspond to the R.I.NA. rules and regulations or to Rules considered equivalent by the R.I.NA. Head Office.

Vessels with the characteristic 2 cannot be used for unlimited services.

Navigation marks

Navigation shall be noted by letters, marks or even by a complete phrase. Generally the following are the navigation marks:

Nav. L = (Navigazione di lungo corso)—Without limits

Nav. G = (Navigazione di Gran cabotaggio)—Great coasting navigation

Nav. P = (Navigazione di Piccolo cabotaggio)—Small coasting navigation

Nav. C = (Navigazione costiera)—Coasting navigation

Nav. I = (Navigazione interna)—Inboard navigation

Nav. S = (Navigazione speciale)—Special navigation (followed by the navigation limits)

Summary

	Ships	Lighters	
		with machinery	without machinery
1st Class	100 A —1.1—Nav.	100 A —1.1	100 A —1
	100 As—1.1—Nav.	100 As—1.1	100 As—1
2nd Class	90 A —1.2—Nav.	90 A —1.2	
	90 A —2.1—Nav.	90 A —2.1	90 A —2
	90 A —2.2—Nav.	90 A —2.2	
	90 As—1.2—Nav.	90 As—1.2	
	90 As—2.1—Nav.	90 As—2.1	90 As—2
	90 As—2.2—Nav.	90 As—2.2	

Symbols of survey during construction

The special symbols of survey during construction are, the

Maltese Cross ✠ and the Star ★. Neither refers to the classification of a vessel.

The symbol Maltese Cross means that the parts of a vessel so recorded have been built under survey, to R.I.NA.'s satisfaction, and according to plans duly approved of. Each of the following parts may be recorded with Maltese Cross:

Hull and equipment

Propelling apparatus, machinery and auxiliaries

Electric installation

Refrigerating installation

A ship shall be recorded with 'star' provided she satisfies to the following conditions:

(1) that the ship had been built under survey and according to plans duly approved of;

(2) that the ship is worthy of classification;

(3) that the materials are as per rules;

(4) that the workmanship is satisfactory;

(5) that:

    (a) the hull and equipment

    (b) the propelling apparatus, machinery and auxiliaries

    (c) the electric installation

    (d) the refrigerating installation

might be recorded ✠ as explained before.

Ships not satisfying to all the aforesaid conditions, shall not be recorded 'star', though built under survey and worthy of classification.

The symbol star is recorded beside the name of a ship and refers to the original conditions of that ship. Said mark shall be cancelled if the ship is transformed or renewed without R.I.NA.'s survey (e.g. if the original propelling machinery has been replaced by another one not properly surveyed by R.I.NA.).

The change of a name of a ship does not affect in any way the symbol 'star'.

Additional notation

A Classification mark may be completed with additional notations regarding service or installations or special arrangements of some kind on board.

Additional notations regarding service, mean that classification has been assigned mainly in connection with that particular service, although the ship may be used also for other service consistent with her type.

Notation for suspension and annulment of classification

The 'suspension of Classification' shall be noted in the 'Register Book' and its Supplements by a black line and date: e.g. 7̲.̲8̲.̲6̲1̲ means class suspended from 7.8.61.

When the classification is cancelled, a notation will be inserted on the 'Register Book' with a double black line: e.g. 7̳.̳8̳.̳6̳1̳ which means classification cancelled from 7.8.61.

Register of Shipping of the USSR. Head Office: Leningrad.
The class of the vessel is denoted by the character:

$$\text{P} \overset{4}{-} \text{C} \atop \text{I} \qquad\qquad \text{or P} \overset{4}{-} \text{C} \atop -$$

indicated in the Classification Certificate issued for the vessel.

The upper figure indicates the number of years between the Periodical Surveys for classification; the lower figure indicates the condition of the equipment of the vessel, e.g. '1' denotes that the equipment of the vessel fully complies with the requirement of the Rules, while a line '–' indicates the presence of certain deviations from the Rules. The letters P and C denote 'Register of Shipping of the USSR'.

Where the hull and main engines (including boilers) are constructed under the supervision of the Register, a mark ✕ is placed in front of the character of the class, thus:

$$\text{✕} \ \text{P} \overset{4}{-} \text{C} \atop \text{I}$$

Where the hull and main engines (including boilers) are not constructed under the supervision of the Register but under the supervision of a foreign Classification Society, the vessel may be assigned the aforementioned supervision mark but with a line underneath, thus:

$$\underset{\underline{}}{X} \quad P \overset{4}{-} \underset{I}{C}$$

Where the hull is constructed under the supervision of the Register but the main engines (including boilers) are built under the supervision of a foreign Classification Society, then the vessel may be assigned the aforementioned mark, but with a dot underneath, thus:

$$\underset{\bullet}{X} \quad P \overset{4}{-} \underset{I}{C}$$

Where a vessel is assigned a freeboard in excess of that which she might receive in accordance with the 'Rules for Assignment of Freeboard', according to her geometrical dimensions, the mark ⊖ is added on the right of the character of the class, thus!

$$X \quad P \overset{4}{-} \underset{I}{C} \ominus$$

If a vessel is intended for navigation in a restricted area, or for special service (e.g. oil tankers, towing vessels, ice-breakers, dredgers, etc.), then an abbreviated description of the restricted area of navigation, or the special service for which the vessel is intended will be affixed, in brackets, to the character of the class.

Vessels having strengthening for navigation with the aid of ice-breakers in broken ice in Southern Seas are assigned a class with the addition of the letter 'Л' prefixed to the original symbol of class, e.g.

$$\text{Л} \times \text{P} \overset{4}{\underset{1}{-}} \text{C} \qquad\qquad \text{Л} \, \text{P} \overset{4}{\underset{1}{-}} \text{C}$$

Vessels having additional strengthening for navigation with the aid of ice-breakers in Northern Seas and for navigation with the aid of ice-breakers in the Arctic Ocean are assigned a class with an addition of the letters 'Y Л' affixed in front of the original symbol of class, thus:

$$\text{Y} \, \text{Л} \, \text{P} \overset{4}{\underset{1}{-}} \text{C}$$

Polish Register of Shipping (PRS). Head Office: Gdansk.
This Classification Society was founded in 1946.
   The principal character of ship's class is distinguished with the following symbols:

$$\text{P} \overset{4}{-} \text{R} \qquad\qquad \text{P} \overset{2}{-} \text{R}$$
$$\text{⚓} \qquad\qquad\qquad \text{⚓}$$

the letters PR stand for 'Polish Register of Shipping'.
   The figure above the line indicates the number of years for which the class has been assigned or renewed. The mark ⚓ signifies that the ship's equipment of anchors, chain cables, towing ropes complies with the Rules. If there is no ⚓ mark in the character but a dash — instead, it means that the equipment does not fully comply with the Rules, but the deviations from the Rules do not deprive the ship of her class.
   A hull built under the PRS special survey during construction is distinguished with a ✳ mark before the principal character of the ship's class.
   Thus the ship's character will be as follows:

$$\underset{\underset{\textstyle\perp}{}}{\ast\,\mathrm{P}\overset{4}{-}\mathrm{R}}\quad\text{or}\quad\underset{\underset{\textstyle\perp}{}}{\ast\,\mathrm{P}\overset{2}{-}\mathrm{R}}$$

If the hull has been built under the special survey during construction of another Classification Society then the survey mark is inserted before the principal character of class but with a dash under it, i.e. $\ast$.

Ships strengthened for navigation in ice have one of the following marks added behind the principal character of class: L1, L2 or L3. These marks signify strengthenings in accordance with the Rules.

A distinguishing mark indicating the zones in which the ship is permitted to trade is inserted behind the principal character of class; the following are the marks of the various zones of navigation:

W—great navigation—unrestricted zone of navigation.
M—small voyage—restricted as in certificate of class.
Bl—navigation in Baltic Sea as in certificate of class.
P—coastal navigation as in certificate of class.

Ships with bulkheads arranged so as to provide sufficient buoyancy and stability under damaged conditions in compliance with the relevant rules have an additional mark 'ı' behind the principal character of class.

Marks for special trade

Ships built to the Rules for ore-carriers have an additional notation 'rud' behind the character of class.

Ships reinforced for carrying ore have 'wr' added behind the character of class.

Ships built to the Rules for tankers have the mark 'zb' behind the character of class.

Ships built to the Rules for passenger ships have the mark 'pas' behind the character of class.

Ships built to the Rules for tugs have the mark 'hol' behind the character of class.

Ships with continous survey have an additional mark 'NS' in parenthesis behind the character of class. Behind the NS mark the abbreviated date (month and year) of the commencement of the continous survey cycle is placed.

Thus as an example:

$$\text{✳ P} \overset{4}{\underset{\text{⚓}}{—}} \text{R W (NS 9.62)}$$

Ships which comply with increased fire safety requirements have the mark 'F' placed behind the principal character of class.

Machinery

The principal character of machinery class is PRM.

The marks ✳ and ✲ are similar to those for the hull.

If the machinery does not fully comply with the Rules but the deviations do not deprive the ship of her class a dash is placed above the principal character for machinery:

$$\text{✳} \ \overline{\text{PRM}}$$

Refrigerated installation

The principal character of class for refrigerating installation is the following:

$$\text{PR Ch}$$

SURVEY

The procedure adopted in dealing with a survey of the hull of a steel ship in the region of 15 years old is given below in a summary form. The description is not that of any particular Classification Society but the items enumerated are those generally inspected at a periodical survey at the age mentioned.

The ship is placed in dry dock or on a slipway, where the blocks are of sufficient height to enable a proper inspection being made of the bottom shell plating. Hold sparring is removed so as to expose the plating to view and allow surfaces to be cleared of rust, cleaned and re-coated. Portions of ceiling in the holds are removed to ascertain condition of steel work.

Any portion of the steel structure where signs of wastage are evident it may be necessary to ascertain, by drilling, the thickness of the material. The comparison between the actual and original thickness will enable a decision to be made as to whether renewal is necessary. Special attention is given to the condition of plating in way of sidelights, rudder, propellers and to all spaces where heat and moisture combine to create corrosion in the plating, framing or riveting.

All steel decks are carefully examined; the condition and thickness of all wood deck and sheathing are noted and if decay or rot is found or the wood excessively worn it is renewed.

The bilges all fore and aft are cleaned and the structure examined. All double bottom and other tanks are cleaned, examined and tested by a head sufficient to give the maximum pressure than can be experienced in service.

The side frames and their end connections at the beams and margin plates are examined and the condition of the structure in the forward and after peaks ascertained. The rudder and rudder post are inspected at the gudgeons and pintles to determine if re-bushing is necessary.

The chain lockers are cleaned and inspected. The chain cables are ranged for inspection and the anchors are examined. If wastage of the cables fall below a specified minimum they are renewed.

The steering engine and all its accessories together with the windlass are examined. Pumps are also tested and sluice and other valves, sounding and air pipes, freeing ports and scuppers are examined.

The condition of the hatchways is of vital importance and all items related thereto are carefully inspected. Strict attention is paid to the means of ensuring watertightness of steel hatch covers.

The freeboard markings are checked with the Certificate.

The main and auxiliary engines and boilers, electrical equipment and refrigerating plant are examined and tested by the appropriate surveyors.

This summary shows that the survey of a ship of the age assumed is very thorough and that on completion of the survey the ship is in a very serviceable condition.

In addition to Statutory Surveys and the Annual and Special Surveys of the Classification Societies a considerable amount of maintenance by the ship's staff is necessary and this requires efficient organisation of maintenance in service to ensure that defects are detected and receive timely attention or are listed for repairs at the end of the voyage. The time and cost for maintenance and repair may be increased many times by poor accessibility. Proper access is essential for effective maintenance.

Most of the expenditure on the upkeep of ships, apart from the running costs, is due to repairs as the result of wastage or on endeavours to minimise it. The protection of the structure against wastage is vital. The principal cause of deterioration of the modern ship arises from corrosion of the steel structure. The scantlings of the parts of the structure known by experience to be specially liable to corrosion are increased. An average corrosion figure for such parts may be from $\frac{4}{1000}$ in to $\frac{6}{1000}$ in per year for a ship's life. Reference to corrosion and its prevention has already been made in Chapter II.

The importance of maintenance in the economics of ships is amply demonstrated by the symposium on 'Ship Maintenance and Associated Design Problems' held by the Royal Institution of Naval Architects in November 1964 and published in the transactions, Volume 107. The papers form a digest of the wide and varied aspects of the policies and problems associated with ship maintenance. The papers presented included Passenger Ships, Cargo Liners and Cargo Tramps, Cross Channel Ships, Oil Tankers.

Ships not built to class

It is usual although not compulsory for a shipowner to have the ship built to the rules of a Classification Society. A ship may be built quite independent of all Society Rules and may ultimately be classed. In such cases the ship is subjected to a complete survey by the Classification Surveyors and after a careful comparison of the structural values of the ship with the standard of the rules a class may be assigned to the ship with the appropriate freeboard. A relatively small number of seagoing ships and also some ships engaged in smooth waters are not classed. If insurance is desired then special arrangements may be concluded between the owners and underwriters. It is not necessary to have a ship classed in order to obtain a load-line assignment in accordance with the statutory rules. In such cases when a load line is desired application is made to the Board of Trade or to an assigning authority. The ship is surveyed and a freeboard assigned in keeping with the standard of strength. These vessels are known as 'unclassed' but this in no way indicates any form of inferiority to classed ships.

Even in the case of unclassed vessels it is not uncommon for the specification to require that the vessel be built to the rule requirements of a particular Classification Society. This clearly indicates that there is universal acceptance of Classification Rules as desirable standards for merchant-ship construction.

V · STABILITY AND TRIM

The amount of water displaced by a vessel afloat is termed the displacement and can be expressed as a volume in cubic feet or as a weight in tons. It is usual to take sea water to weigh 64 lb per cu ft which is equivalent to 35 cu ft to the ton. The corresponding figures for fresh water are 62·3 lb per cu ft and 36 cu ft to the ton.

There are three conditions which must be fulfilled in order that a ship may float freely and at rest in stable equilibrium.

(1) The weight of the water displaced must equal the total weight of the ship.
(2) The centre of gravity (G) of the ship must be in the same vertical line as the centre of buoyancy (B).
(3) The centre of gravity must be below the transverse metacentre (M).

When a ship is inclined from a position of rest by an external force, such as the effect of wave motion or wind pressure, the vessel exerts a resistance to oppose this external force. The forces which tend to incline the ship are dynamic and the opposing force exerted by the ship is static. While the ship is at sea these forces are in constant operation and opposition; if the dynamic forces exceed the static the ship will capsize. The moment of force which is exerted to restore the ship to the upright after inclination is the measure of the ship's stability. This static power of the ship is dealt with later in this chapter.

The total weight of the ship (W) is assumed to be concentrated at its centre of gravity (G). The supporting forces exerted by the water in which the ship is floating act at right-angles to the surface of the shell plating, and the resultant of all these forces, which is called the buoyancy, may be considered as acting upwards through a point B which is known as the centre of buoyancy. This is shown in Figure 37. The weight and the buoyancy of the ship are equal.

Thus the following forces act upon the ship:

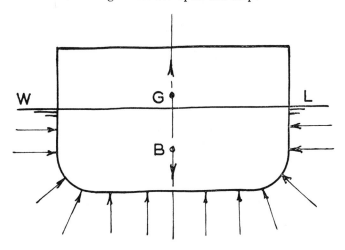

37 Centre of buoyancy and centre of gravity

(a) The weight (W) acting downwards through the centre of gravity (G).
(b) The buoyancy (W) acting upwards through the centre of buoyancy (B).

For the ship to be at rest these two forces must act in the same line and counteract each other. This is condition 2 as stated above.

A simple illustration of the foregoing is as follows: If a rope is pulled at both ends by men exerting the same strength the rope will, obviously, remain stationary. This is the case of a ship floating freely and at rest in still water.

Transverse metacentre

Figure 38 shows the section of a ship steadily inclined at a small

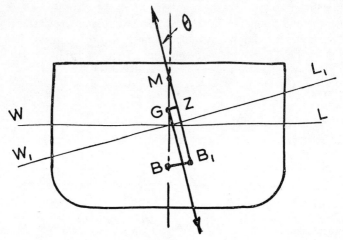

38 Ship inclined at small angle

angle from the upright by some external force such as the wind. The waterline in the upright is WL and on being inclined W_1L_1. The volume of displacement remains the same after inclination as before so that the wedge-shaped volume represented by WSW_1 which has emerged from the water is equal to the volume of LSL_1 which is immersed.

It is assumed that no weights on board shift and consequently the centre of gravity remains in the same position in the ship. Although the total volume of displacement remains the same, the shape of this volume changes, and hence the centre of buoyancy shifts from its original position and moves out in the same direction as the inclination to a point B_1. The upward force of buoyancy acts vertically through B_1 so that there are now two forces not acting in the same vertical line. Such a system of forces is termed a couple.

The point M where the vertical line passing through B_1, the new position of the centre of buoyancy, intersects the vertical line passing through B, the original centre of buoyancy, is termed the transverse metacentre. This point M is assumed fixed for angles of inclination up to about 15 degrees. For large angles of inclination the metacentre does not remain fixed.

The distance between G and the vertical line of buoyancy through B_1 is GZ. This distance is the arm of the couple referred to above, and the moment of the couple is W × GZ which is called the moment of statical stability. From Figure 38 it will be seen that the couple is tending to take the ship back to the upright. Thus when M is above G the GZ is a righting lever. When these points coincide the ship is in neutral equilibrium and when G is above M the lever is an upsetting one. This shows how important the relative positions of the centre of gravity and the transverse metacentre arc as affecting a ship's initial stability. The distance GM is termed the transverse metacentric height, or, generally, simply the metacentric height.

For small angles of heel M remains, more or less, in a constant position, and so GZ = GM sin Ø for angles up to about 15 degrees. So the moment of statical stability at small angles from the upright can be written as : W × GM sin Ø; W being the weight of the ship in tons and Ø the angle of inclination in degrees.

Consequently the moment tending to right the ship is directly dependent on GM. The distance GM, the metacentric height, is taken as the measure of initial stability of a ship at small angles of heel.

A ship with a large GM comes back to the upright very quickly after being inclined and may be uncomfortable. A large GM is not desired when the ship is fully loaded as this may cause the cargo to shift with disastrous results. Such a vessel is said to be stiff. A vessel with a small GM and which is inclined easily to a large angle of heel is called a tender ship. For steadiness in a seaway the metacentric height must be small. There are thus two opposing conditions to fulfil:

(1) The metacentric height must be enough to allow the ship to resist inclination by external forces.

(2) The metacentric height must be moderate enough to make the ship steady in a seaway.

In cargo ships the conditions are continually changing due to the varying nature and the distribution of the cargo carried. It is considered that in cargo ships the minimum value of GM in the worst condition of loading should be about 1 ft.

For passenger ships, comfort at sea is very important, and it is desirable that such ships should not have a metacentric height of over 5 per cent of the breadth for vessels of 50 ft breadth, and not over 6 per cent of the breadth for vessels of about 100 ft breadth.

The position of the centre of buoyancy and the metacentre together with the displacement and other items are calculated for various draughts by the shipyard design staff and presented in the form of curves in what is known as the Hydrostatic Curves. A modified form of such curves is shown in Figure 39. From these curves or from a tabular statement derived from them the ship's officers can readily obtain the position of the centre of buoyancy, metacentre and other items for any condition of loading.

The foregoing deals with the stability of a ship at small angles of inclination but it is essential to have details of the actual stability of the ship when inclined to large angles of heel. This further information is given by a curve of stability (known as a 'curve of statical stability') and is prepared by the shipyard design staff. A typical curve of statical stability is shown in Figure 40.

In the calculations for the curve of statical stability it is assumed that the centre of gravity remains in the same position in the ship at all angles of heel. However, the length of the righting lever, GZ, varies as the angle of heel increases and these are calculated and plotted as shown in Figure 40. Usually GZ gradually increases until an angle is reached when it obtains a maximum value. This angle is termed the angle of maximum stability. On further inclination an angle will be reached when GZ becomes zero, the curve crosses the base line. The point where this takes place is termed the angle of vanishing stability or range of stability. Beyond this point GZ becomes negative and the couple W × GZ no longer tends to right the ship but is an upsetting couple tending to incline the ship still further. The lengths of the

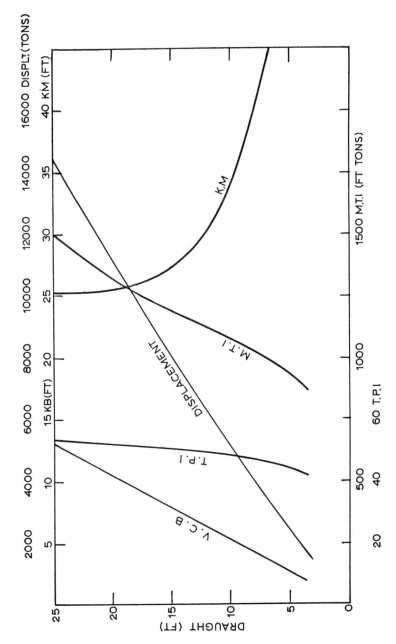

39 Hydrostatic curves

righting levers are calculated for a particular condition, that is, for a definite displacement and vertical position of the centre of gravity. If any alteration takes place in these factors then a new or modified curve is necessary.

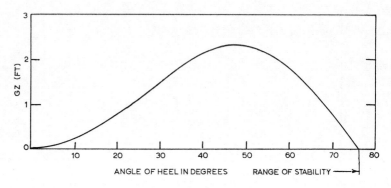

40 Curve of statical stability

The transverse stability of a ship is influenced by the dimensions principally the breadth and draught and also by the vertical position of the centre of gravity. The breadth has a direct effect on initial stability, the greater the breadth the more it will increase the height of the metacentre. A change in draught automatically changes the freeboard. An increase of freeboard has no effect on initial stability but it has a most important effect in increasing the range of stability. The greater the freeboard the larger will be the angle of inclination before the deck edge is awash.

The centre of gravity has a direct influence on stability. If the centre of gravity is raised then the righting lever GZ at any angle Ø is diminished by the amount raised multiplied by sin Ø. For example if the centre of gravity is raised 2 ft then the GZ at the angle 30 degrees is diminished by 1 ft. For 30 degrees sin $Ø = \frac{1}{2}$. In a particular case of a ship of 10,000 tons displacement the raising of the centre of gravity by 2 ft reduced the range of stability by 12 degrees.

The position of the metacentre above the centre of buoyancy

(BM) is obtained by dividing the moment of inertia (I) of the waterplane by the volume of displacement. That is $BM = I/V$.

In the case of a waterplane each element of area is supposed multiplied by the square of its distance from the desired axis and the sum of all these products is the moment of inertia of the entire waterplane. Consequently an increase in the breadth of a ship increases the moment of inertia. If the displacement of the ship is increased by say the addition of cargo or fuel then the distance between the centre of buoyancy (B) and the metacentre (M) is reduced.

The vertical position of the centre of gravity of the ship depends upon the vertical distribution of the weights forming the structure and the loading of the ship. The position of the metacentre depends solely upon the form of the ship and can be determined when the geometrical form of the underwater portion of the ship is known.

When a ship is in the lightship or lightweight condition the centre of gravity is in a certain position relative to the keel. The lightship condition is the ship complete and ready for sea but no fuel, water, ballast, cargo, passengers on board. The position of the centre of gravity in this condition is taken as the basis of assessment of the position of G for any other condition, say when cargo or fuel is added. The total deadweight of a ship is the difference between the load displacement and the lightweight, and the deadweight thus includes fuel, water, ballast, cargo and passengers.

The ship's officer has no control over the factors affecting stability in the lightship condition but he can considerably influence the stability by the distribution of cargo when the ship is being loaded. The initial effect, in general, when loading a ship is to lower the centre of gravity since the centre of gravity of the added cargo will be below the initial position of G of the ship. As the loading proceeds the centre of gravity will rise. It is thus essential to keep heavy loads low down in the ship and light loads in the tween decks. It is the disposition of cargo which can have a direct effect in making a ship stiff or tender.

The Rules of the International Convention respecting Load Lines, 1966, makes it a condition of assignment of freeboard that:

The master of every new ship shall be supplied with sufficient information, in an approved form, to enable him to arrange for the loading and ballasting of his ship in such a way as to avoid the creation of any unacceptable stresses in the ship's structure.

The Regulations assume that the nature and stowage of the cargo, ballast, etc., are such as to secure sufficient stability of the ship.

It is common practice to supply to the ship a statement of draughts, trims and metacentric heights for several different conditions of loading, together with sets of statical stability curves for such conditions. These conditions include both departure and arrival conditions as frequently the arrival condition is the one in which stability is least. This is because fuel, water and stores have been consumed and, in general, the metacentric height has been reduced.

These statements of stability are very valuable for general guidance. A ship's master and his officers must be able to maintain a considerable measure of control over the stability of their ship. Knowledge of stability is part of the professional equipment of an officer in the mercantile marine.

If as the result of the motion of the ship at sea the cargo shifts a very dangerous situation could arise. The centre of gravity of the ship moves with the angle of inclination, creating a permanent list, and this may have a serious effect upon the stability of the ship. It is because of this that special precautions are taken with such cargoes as grain in bulk, oil in bulk, etc., by fitting shifting boards, longitudinal bulkheads, or other equivalent means of restricting the transverse movement of cargo.

Free surface

Another very important matter is the effect of a free surface of water or oil on the stability of a ship. A compartment which is partly filled with a liquid permits a free surface within the compartment. The effect of free surfaces is to reduce the actual value of the metacentric height (GM). The amount of water or liquid does not affect the result but only the moment of inertia of the free surface. The quantity of liquid, like the displacement, remains unchanged as the ship heels. In each case the upper boundary is a horizontal surface. The weight of the liquid, like the force of buoyancy, always acts vertically.

Assume that the centre of gravity of the ship, with water having a free surface in a double bottom tank, is situated at G, and the metacentre is at M, as shown in Figure 41. If the ship is inclined,

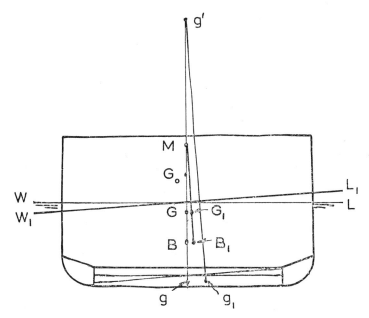

41 Free surface

the water in the tank will adjust itself so that its surface is parallel to the level waterline W_1L_1. The centre of gravity of the water in the double bottom tank will move with the inclination to a point g_1 and its effect is as if the water acted as a weight attached to a pendulum pivoted at g^1. This is the point where the vertical through g_1 intersects the vertical through G of the ship in the upright position. This point is termed the *virtual* centre of gravity of the water. This has the same effect as placing a weight at g^1 some distance above G and the result is to raise G to G_0 and consequently reduce the distance between G and M the metacentric height.

The rise in G or, what is the same thing, the reduction in the metacentric height is given by dividing the moment of inertia of the surface of the water in the double bottom space by the volume of displacement of the ship:

that is $\qquad GG_0 = \dfrac{i}{V}$

If the free surface is rectangular in shape then the moment of inertia is given by: $i = \dfrac{1}{12} Ah^2$ where A is the area of free surface in sq ft; h is the transverse dimension of the free surface in ft. So that it can be written:

$$\frac{i}{V} = \frac{\text{length of tank in ft} \times (\text{breadth of tank in ft})^3}{\text{Volume of displacement in cu ft} \times 12}$$

For example: In a ship of 8000 tons displacement there is a tank 45 ft long and 40 ft broad. The tank contains water which is free to move and thus has a free surface. The loss of metacentric height due to the free surface is

$$\frac{i}{V} = \frac{45 \times 40^3}{8000 \times 35 \times 12} = 0.86 \text{ ft}$$

It is thus important to have all tanks empty or filled to prevent free surface. It will also be appreciated that it is a dangerous operation to fill a ballast tank at sea in heavy weather.

Inclining experiment

It is required by law that every new ship must be inclined upon its completion and the elements of stability determined. The immediate purpose of the inclining experiment is to determine the metacentric height. The ultimate purpose is to ascertain the height of the centre of gravity for a definite condition of the ship —the light condition. This height is of great importance in design work and in the calculations for the different loading conditions.

The method of conducting an inclining experiment is as follows:

Suitable known weights are placed on the upper deck as near

the sides of the ship as possible and the distance from centre to centre of these weights measured as shown in Figure 42. Two plumb lines are suspended at convenient places such as through an open hatchway. Some distance below the point of suspension is fixed a horizontal batten upon which is indicated the shift of

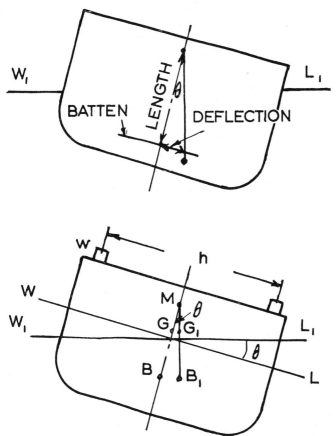

42 Inclining experiment

the plumb-line during inclination. Each pendulum should be as long as possible and consists of a fine piano wire supporting a heavy bob. With the ship in the upright position the position of

I

the plumb-line is marked on the batten. The weights on the upper deck are then moved transversely across the deck and vice versa and readings of the movement of the pendulum after each shift of the weights indicated on the batten. This process is repeated several times and a mean of the readings used in the calculation. The inclination is sometimes measured by an instrument called a stabilograph which records directly the movement of the ship by means of an ink line on a piece of paper marked in degrees.

When the upper deck weights (w) are moved through a distance h (Figure 42) the centre of gravity of the ship G moves to G_1 and the centre of buoyancy B moves to B_1. Vertical lines through these two points pass through M the metacentre.

The shift of G to G_1 is given by $\dfrac{w \times h}{W}$ where W is the displacement of the ship in tons. GG_1 is parallel to the movement of w and thus the angle MGG_1 is 90 degrees.

If Ø is the angle of inclination of the ship, the tangent of the angle is perpendicular $\div$ base

$$\text{thus } \tan \varnothing = \frac{GG_1}{GM} \quad \text{also } \tan \varnothing = \frac{\text{deflection of pendulum}}{\text{length of pendulum}}$$

$$GM = \frac{GG_1}{\tan \varnothing} = \frac{w \times h}{W} \times \frac{\text{length of pendulum}}{\text{deflection of pendulum}}$$

Example. In a ship of 6000 tons displacement a weight of 5 tons is moved across the deck a distance of 50 ft. The deflection of the pendulum at 25 ft below the point of suspension was 6 in. The value of the GM is desired for this condition.

$$GM = \frac{wh}{W} \times \frac{\text{length}}{\text{deflection}}$$

$$= \frac{5 \times 50}{6000} \times \frac{25 \times 12}{6} = 2 \cdot 1 \text{ ft}$$

The following precautions should be taken in performing an inclining experiment.

(1) A calm day should be selected in order to obtain conditions that will not affect the accuracy of the readings.

(2) All main tanks should be empty or pressed full.

(3) The ship should be free to incline. Gangways off and moorings slack.

(4) The ship should be upright.

(5) All loose weights such as derricks and boats should be secured.

(6) Draughts forward and aft should be read and the density of the water ascertained.

The position of M can always be obtained from the 'Hydrostatic Curves', Figure 39, or from the 'Metacentric Diagram', Figure 43. The metacentric diagram is a graph showing the variation in the height of the metacentre with variation in draught. One method of plotting is shown in Figure 43. Here a line is drawn through the origin at 45 degrees, and waterlines are drawn to cut this sloping line. At the intersection of the waterline and the 45 degree line a vertical line is drawn, and on this vertical the corresponding height of M is set up. This is equivalent to setting off the draughts both horizontally and vertically. The calculated position of the metacentre above the centre of buoyancy at the different waterlines is set up. The latter being given above the keel (KB). So that the position of the metacentre above the keel (KM) can be readily obtained. By deducting the value of GM determined from the inclining experiment the position of the centre of gravity of the ship above the keel (KG) for the inclined condition is available as shown in Figure 44.

Frequently the height of the ship's centre of gravity for certain definite conditions of loading are given on the metacentric diagram. There are, for example, the light condition, the deep load departure condition with homogeneous cargo, and the deep load arrival condition with fuel and stores consumed.

As the ship is generally in an incomplete condition at the time of the inclining experiment, it is necessary to take an accurate account of all weights to go on board to complete with their positions in the ship together with a record of all weights to be

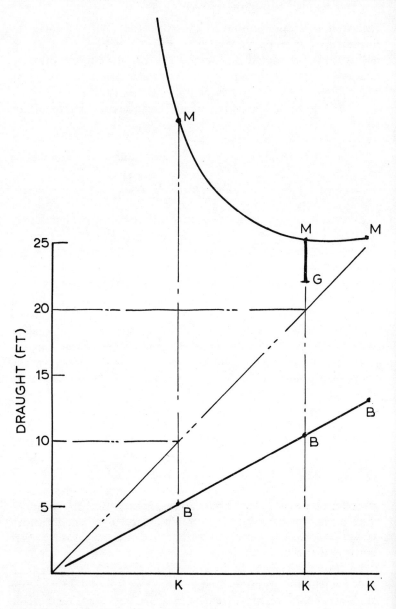

43 Metacentric diagram

removed with their positions. The effect these weights have on the centre of gravity already determined is calculated and the final position of the KG for the ship in the light ship condition is obtained.

$$KM = KB + BM$$
$$KG = KM - GM$$

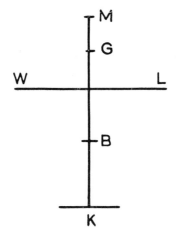

44 Derivation of KG

Stabilisers

In recent years there has been quite an increase in the number of ships fitted with some form of stabilising or roll damping device. Roll stabilisation systems can be passive or active. Passive stabilisers are self-acting and may be regarded as damping or resisting the motion rather than providing a positive stabilising action.

Active stabilisers depend for their action on some external source of power and require a control system. The most highly developed of the active stabilisers is the activated-fin type. These are repre-

sented by the Motora and the Denny-Brown. Both types consist
of fins shaped rather like a balanced rudder. The Denny-Brown
is retractable in housings within the vessel. The fins are arranged
to tilt through an angle of about 20 degrees. With the ship rolling
to port, the port fin is inclined downwards from the leading edge
and the starboard fin upwards. Each fin thus contributes a
stablising moment. On a roll to starboard, the slope of the fin is
reversed. In practice, fins are normally designed to give a roll
reduction of about 90 per cent.

Trim

Trim is the longitudinal inclination of a ship. It is measured by
the difference between the forward and after draughts. A ship is
said to be on an even keel when the draughts are the same forward
and aft. A ship is said to be 'down by the head' when the draught
forward is greater than the draught aft, and 'down by the stern'
when the draught aft is greater.

The draught marks are generally placed on the stem and sternpost and are made so that their vertical projection is 6 in and the
intervening space also 6 in. The bottom of the figure corresponds
with the waterline measurement.

Change of trim (t) is the sum of the change of draughts forward
and aft and in Figure 45 is $WW_1 + LL_1$ and is also equal to length

of ship $\times \tan \emptyset$, the angle of trim. That is $\tan \emptyset = \dfrac{t.}{L}$ When a ship

changes trim without change in displacement the vessel turns about
a transverse axis through the centre of flotation (F). The centre of
flotation is the centre of the area of the waterplane. This means
that the draught at F will remain unchanged so long as the displacement is unchanged. If F is 'abaft' amidships, the
changes of draught will be greater forward than aft, and vice
versa. As the centre of flotation is never far from amidships the
difference will not be great and as an approximation it can be
taken that the changes forward and aft will be equal and each
equal to one-half the change in trim.

A change of trim can be brought about by moving weights
already on board in a fore and aft direction. In Figure 45 the

vessel floats at waterline WL with the weight w on board. Suppose the weight w be shifted forward a distance d feet. Then G the original position of the ship's centre of gravity will move forward parallel to the line joining the original and final positions of w

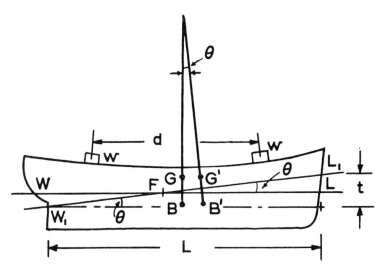

45 Trim and change of trim

and if W is the displacement of the ship, G will move to G^1 such that $GG^1 = \dfrac{w \times d}{W}$

w × d is called the trimming moment.

Because of this shift of w the centre of gravity and the centre of buoyancy will not be in the same vertical line and consequently the ship will adjust to a new waterline W_1L_1 so that the centre of gravity and centre of buoyancy are in the same vertical line. The new centre of buoyancy being B^1. The original vertical through B and G meets the new vertical through B^1 and G^1 in the point M_L and this point is known as the longitudinal metacentre and for small changes of trim GM_L is the longitudinal metacentric height.

$$\text{Also } \tan \emptyset = \frac{GG^1}{GM_L}$$

Now

$$\tan \emptyset = \frac{t}{L} \text{ also } \tan \emptyset = \frac{GG^1}{GM_L}$$

$$\text{thus } t/L = \frac{GG^1}{GM_L} = \frac{w \times d}{W \times GM_L}$$

or t the change of trim due to the trimming moment w × d

$$= \frac{w \times d}{W \times GM_L} \text{ L ft}$$

thus the change of trim in inches $= \dfrac{w \times d \times L \times 12}{W \times GM_L}$

and the moment to change 1 in (MTI) is the value of w × d which gives a result = 1

$$\text{Hence MTI} = \frac{W \times GM_L}{12L} \text{ tons ft}$$

A convenient approximation to MTI is given by the expression

$$\text{MTI} = \frac{3 \text{ } 1 \text{ } T^2}{B} \text{ tons ft}$$

where T = tons per inch immersion and B = breath of ship in ft.

The shipowner, master and officers are concerned with the results of hydrostatic calculations particularly within the range of draught from the draught at which the ship floats in the light-ship condition to the maximum draught permitted by load line regulations. One of these results with which the shipowner, master and officers are concerned is the deadweight. Since the deadweight at any draught is the difference between the dis-placement at that draught and the light displacement, the variation of deadweight with draught could be expressed in the form of a curve. However a more convenient form expresses the variation of deadweight with draught in tabular form. A typical deadweight scale is shown in Figure 46; it shows in addition to the dead-weight a scale of tons per in. immersion since this is of very great interest to masters and officers.

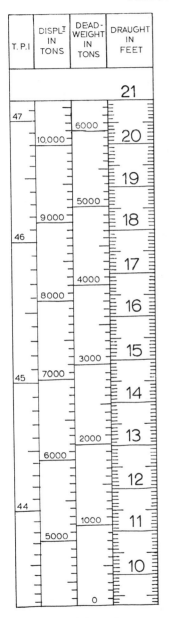

T. P.I	DISPL.ᵗ IN TONS	DEAD-WEIGHT IN TONS	DRAUGHT IN FEET

46 Deadweight scale

It is customary to associate the deadweight scale, supplied for the use of the ship's officers, with a 'capacity plan'. This is generally a small scale profile on which are indicated the location and capacities of the cargo spaces, fuel tanks, fresh water tanks and water-ballast tanks. Generally schedules of the capacities of the cargo holds are given for different purposes, namely grain and bale. A typical example is given in Table 2 for a passenger-cargo ship. The cargo space volume for grain, which can flow right out to the sides of the ship, is measured to the inside of the shell and the underside of the deck. For 'bale' measurement which indicates the space is available for the stowage of cargo in bales or cases, the volume is measured to the inside of hold sparring and below the beams. For an ordinary cargo space the grain figure is about 8 to 10 per cent greater than the bale figure.

It is essential that the information be available, for the ship's master and officers to estimate trim as well as stability. It may, for example, be necessary from the draughts at a departure port to estimate the draughts on arrival at the next, making allowance for the consumption of fuel and water during the voyage. In view of this it is usual to associate with the deadweight scale tabulated values of moment to change trim one inch over a range of draughts. The desired information is sometimes presented in tabular form showing the changes of draught brought about by filling or emptying each ballast and fuel tank, and the changes resulting from adding 100 tons at the centre of each cargo compartment. Typical examples are given in Tables 2 and 3. These values can

TABLE 2

CARGO CAPACITIES

COMPARTMENT	GRAIN (cubic ft)	BALE (cubic ft)	CHANGE OF DRAUGHT (ins) DUE TO ADDING 100 TONS CARGO	
			Forward	Aft
No. 1 Hold	32900	27500	$+8\frac{3}{4}$	-4
No. 1 'Tween Dk.	17600	14800	$+8\frac{1}{2}$	-4
No. 1 Trunked Hatch	3800	3680	$+9$	$-4\frac{1}{4}$
No. 2 Hold	71100	65900	$+6\frac{1}{4}$	$-1\frac{3}{4}$
No. 2 Tween Dk.	38950	33300	$+6\frac{1}{4}$	$-1\frac{3}{4}$
No. 2 Trunked Hatch	10300	10050	$+7$	$-2\frac{1}{4}$
No. 3 Hold	25680	20350	$+4$	0
No. 4 Hold	32300	27850	$-2\frac{1}{4}$	$+5\frac{3}{4}$
No. 4 Tween Dk.	29450	26250	$-2\frac{1}{4}$	$+5\frac{3}{4}$
No. 4 Trunked Hatch	8800	8500	$-2\frac{3}{4}$	$+6\frac{1}{4}$
No. 5 Hold	15700	12600	-4	$+7\frac{1}{2}$
No. 5 'Tween Dk.	21300	18350	-4	$+7\frac{1}{2}$
No. 5 Trunked Hatch	7250	7000	$-4\frac{1}{2}$	$+7\frac{3}{4}$
Total	315130	276130		

only be given for one draught and to simplify matters the draught chosen for the calculation is at a little more than the mean between the light and load draughts.

The effect on the draught of a ship when an amount of cargo is (a) moved from one position on board to another, (b) added, is illustrated by two simple examples.

(a) At an even keel draught of 21 ft a ship has an MTI of 950 tons ft. Determine the effect on the draught when a weight of 100 tons already on board is moved forward a distance of 190 ft.

Trimming moment = 100 × 190 tons ft.

$$\text{Total trim} = \frac{\text{trimming moment}}{\text{MTI}} = \frac{100 \times 190}{950} = 20 \text{ in.}$$

Assuming that the centre of flotation (F) of the waterplane is at amidships then change of draught aft and forward is $\frac{20}{2} = 10$ in.

So that the resulting draughts will be:
Aft: 21 ft 0 in − 10 in = 20 ft 2 in
Forward: 21 ft 0 in + 10 in = 21 ft 10 in

TABLE 3 OIL FUEL

COMPARTMENT		TONS	CHANGE OF DRAUGHT (ins) WHEN FILLING EACH TANK	
			Forward	Aft
No. 3 D.B. Tank	Cr	80	+3¼	0
No. 3 Tank	P & S	175	+7	0
No. 4 D. B. Tank	CR	130	+2½	+2½
No. 4 D.B. Tank	P & S	230	+2½	+2¼
Deep Tank Forward	P & S	220	+7	+2
Deep Tank Aft	P & S	220	+5½	+3½
Settling Tanks	P & S	50	0	+2
Total		1105		

BALLAST AND FRESH WATER TANKS

Fore Peak	W. B.	75	+7¾	−4
No. 1 D.B.	W. B.	170	+14¾	−7
No. 2 D.B. F.W.	P & S	310	+19	−5½
No. 5 D.B. F.W.	P & S	170	−½	+7
No. 6 D.B. F.W.	P & S	120	−2½	+6½
No. 7 D.B. F.W.		25	−1	+1¾
Wing Tanks F.W.	P & S	160	−1½	+7
Aft Peak	W. B.	100	−5¾	+9

(b) A ship of length 380 ft floats on even keel at 20 ft draught. At this draught the TPI is 40, the centre of flotation (F) is 10 ft abaft amidships and the MTI is 900 tons ft. Determine the draughts when a weight of 300 tons is placed on board with its centre of gravity 90 ft abaft amidships.

This type of problem is solved in two steps.

(1) Assume weight placed in line with F so that ship sinks bodily without trimming.

(2) Move weight from F to the desired position. This will cause ship to trim and the trimming moment lever is measured from F.

Thus (1) Parallel sinkage $= \dfrac{300}{40} = 7\cdot5$ in.

$\quad$ (2) Trimming lever $= 90 - 10 = 80$ ft.
$\quad\quad$ Trimming moment $= 300 \times 80$ tons ft.

Total trim $= \dfrac{300 \times 80}{900} = 26\cdot7$ in.

The proportion of the change of trim either aft or forward is the proportion the length of the vessel abaft or forward of the centre of flotation bears to the length of the ship.

$\quad\quad$ Thus trim forward $= 26\cdot7 \times \dfrac{200}{380} = 14\cdot1$ in.

$\quad\quad\quad\quad$ aft $= 26\cdot7 \times \dfrac{180}{380} = 12\cdot6$ in.

So that	Draught aft	Draught forward
	20 ft 0 in	20 ft 0 in
Sinkage	$+7\cdot5$ in	$+7\cdot5$ in
Trim	$+12\cdot6$ in	$-14\cdot1$ in
	21 ft 8·1 in	19 ft 5·4 in
say	21 ft 8 in	19 ft 5½ in

Draught

The depth moulded is the depth of the ship at amidships from top of keel to the top of deck beam at side of the ship. The name of the deck to which the depth is measured should always be stated. The draught of a ship is the distance of the lowest point of the keel below the waterline. Moulded draught is the distance to top of keel below the waterline.

The maximum draught of a ship to the centre of the freeboard disc, marked on the sides of the ship, which is the summer mark, is obtained by adding to the moulded depth the thickness of the stringer plate on the freeboard deck, together with the thickness of any sheathing on the exposed freeboard deck; from this total is deducted the summer freeboard. The result is the 'summer' moulded draught and to obtain the extreme draught the thickness of the keel has to be added.

In the Register Book of Lloyd's Register of Shipping there is recorded, for every ship to which the Classification Society has assigned a freeboard, particulars of the moulded depth to the freeboard deck, the actual summer freeboard, and the extreme summer draught.

The following is an example of how the extreme summer draught is determined.

	ft	in
Moulded depth to freeboard deck	32	0
Thickness of stringer plate		$\frac{3}{4}$
No sheathing on freeboard deck		
	32 —	$0\frac{3}{4}$
Summer freeboard	6 —	$8\frac{1}{2}$
Summer moulded draught	25 —	$4\frac{1}{4}$
Thickness of keel		2
Extreme summer draught	25 —	$6\frac{1}{4}$

Frequently it is necessary to assess the decrease in draught which will take place when a vessel proceeds to sea from a loading port where the water is fresh or partly so. This is to ensure that when at sea the vessel will not be loaded beyond the summer or winter freeboard marks as applicable. The fresh water, unit density, allowance under the load line rules is obtained by the expression: $\dfrac{\triangle}{40\,T}$ in where $\triangle =$ displacement in sea water in tons at the summer load line.

$T=$ tons per inch immersion in sea water at the summer load line. So that for a ship where $\triangle =$ 12,000 tons and $T=$ 40, the fresh water, unit density, allowance is

$$\frac{12,000}{40 \times 40} = 7\cdot5 \text{ in.}$$

The density of fresh water is 1000 oz to the cu ft and that of sea water is taken as 1025 oz, the difference being 25 oz. The density of the water at the various ports will vary according to locality and even according to the state of the tide. Thus at Dundee the water is 1021 oz per cu ft at high water and 1006 oz at low water.

Assume a ship is loading at a port where the density of the water is 1008 oz to the cubic foot and the fresh water load line is 7·5 in above the centre of the disc, the difference between the density of the water at the loading port and that of sea water is 17 oz. The increase beyond the centre of the freeboard disc to which the vessel can be loaded before leaving the port will be $\dfrac{17}{25} \times 7\cdot5$ in which is equal to 5·1 in, say 5 in. This means that on arrival in sea water the ship will then be floating at the permissible draught to the centre of disc.

VI · TONNAGE AND FREEBOARD

TONNAGE

The measurement of tonnage is an economic problem. Tonnage is one of the very important subjects associated with the shipping industry and has, in fact, been directly responsible for the creation of several ship types. The principle upon which British tonnage measurements is based has been the subject of considerable controversy for generations. Broadly the principle is to assess the taxable capacity of a ship according to its internal volume. The regulations are rather complex and their application rather confusing to many people whose interests are closely allied to the operation of ships.

The earliest record in Britain having reference to tonnage is in the year 1422 when a Government law stipulated that vessels that carry coals had to be measured and marked; no reference was made as to how this was to be carried out. It has been suggested that the term 'tonnage' came into use when the dues then charged were based on the number of casks of wine or 'tuns' that a vessel could carry. The 'tun' at that time was a legal standard measurement such that a tun of wine was to measure not less than 252 gallons. It thus appears that internal capacity and not weight was the basis of the first system of tonnage measurement.

Over the years commissions were appointed and formulated rules for tonnage. A Royal Commission was appointed in 1849 with a George Moorsom as its secretary and they introduced new tonnage laws which were embodied in the Merchant Shipping Act of 1854. This became known as the 'Moorsom System' on which all the tonnage laws and regulations of most maritime nations are still based today.

The method of calculating tonnage and the details of tonnage are contained in *Instructions as to the Tonnage Measurement of Ships*, published by H.M. Stationery Office.

As is apparent from the diagrams in the official instructions the rules were originally intended for wood ships. The loss of volume with the heavy wood timbers was so large that all tonnage measurements were taken as inside dimensions; the same applies today as the dimensions are taken within sparring and ceiling.

In the regulations which govern the measurement of ships the tonnage is one of capacity, the unit of one ton being a capacity measurement of 100 cu ft. Simply, the Act was based on the internal volume of the ship in cu ft divided by an easy divisor, the figure 100 was selected. The unit of 100 cu ft is known as the register ton, since the final assessment has to be registered. The tonnage laws provide for two measurements of tonnage, the 'gross' and the 'net'. The former requires an initial measurement in what is known as the 'under-deck' tonnage. Port charges and canal dues are generally levied on the 'net' tonnage. Dry dock, towing charges and other fees are usually based on the 'gross' tonnage. The net tonnage as the basis for the assessment of dues for services rendered to a ship has been the subject of considerable controversy for generations.

UNDER-DECK TONNAGE

Tonnage deck

This is defined as the upper deck in all ships which have less than three decks and the second deck from below in all other ships. The tonnage length is taken on the tonnage deck from a point forward at the stem where the inside surfaces of the frames or sparring, if fitted, intersect to a similar point aft at the stern. The tonnage length is then divided into a number of stations in accordance with the length of the ship. At each of these stations the depth of hold is measured from the top of ceiling, if fitted, to the top of the beams under the tonnage deck, less one-third of the round of beam. Each of the tonnage depths is divided into a number of parts as defined in the regulations. At each of the divisions the breadths of the ship are measured to the inside surface of the sparring if fitted, or to the inside surface of the frames if sparring is not fitted. The area of each transverse station is then calculated and Simpson's rule applied to the areas; this gives the volume of the ship under the tonnage deck which when divided by 100 will give the total under deck tonnage below the tonnage deck. The double bottom spaces are excluded on the condition that these spaces are not used for the carriage of cargo.

The measurements of the length, breadths and depths for under-deck tonnage are shown in Figure 47.

GROSS TONNAGE

This is the under-deck tonnage, together with 'tween deck spaces and all enclosed spaces above including excess of hatchways. Any excess over one-half per cent of the gross tonnage is included. Allowance is made for spaces which are exempt from measurement. The spaces with temporary means of closing openings are those involved in the controversy mentioned above.

A new system, the 'tonnage mark system' has been put forward by Inter-Governmental Maritime Consultative Organisation, IMCO, and details of this are given later in this chapter.

NET TONNAGE

The net tonnage is the amount that remains after certain approved deductions have been made from the gross tonnage. These deductions are broadly:
(a) propelling power allowance
(b) items under section 79 of the Merchant Shipping Act (MSA)

(a) *Propelling power allowance.* The engine-room tonnage may include the following:
(1) Space below the crown of the engine room

K

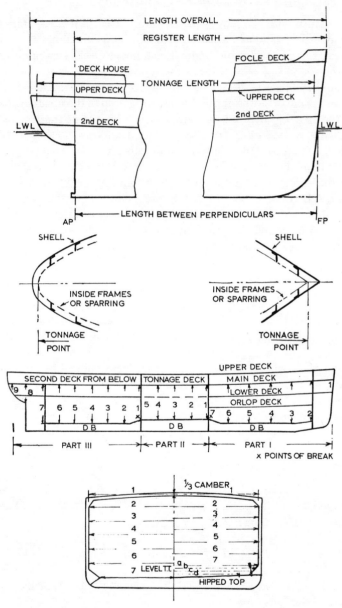

47 Tonnage dimensions

(2) Space between the crown and the upper deck, framed in for machinery or for the admission of light and air.

(3) Space similarly framed in above the upper deck.

(4) The contents of the shaft tunnel or tunnels.

If light and air spaces above the crown of the machinery space are included in the measurement of the engine room then they must be included in the gross tonnage; whole spaces must be used not just portions of a space. Figure 48 is a typical instance of light and air spaces above the machinery space.

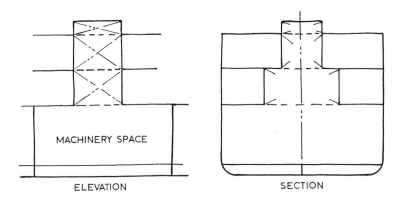

MACHINERY SPACE

ELEVATION   SECTION

48 Light and air spaces

The propelling power allowance for British tonnage is determined by special rules depending upon the size of the engine room.

(1) When the tonnage of the actual engine room amounts to above 13 per cent and under 20 per cent of the gross tonnage of the ship, the allowance is 32 per cent of the gross tonnage.

(2) If the tonnage is 13 per cent of the gross tonnage of the ship the allowance is 32 per cent of the gross. If the tonnage is less than 13 per cent the allowance is 32 per cent of the gross tonnage proportionately reduced. Thus if engine room is 11 per cent of gross the allowance is $\frac{11}{13} \times 32$ per cent. Prior to 1954 no proportional reduction was allowed. The amended Act improves the position with regard to small engine rooms.

(3) If the tonnage is 20 per cent or more of the gross, the allow-

ance may be 32 per cent of the gross or alternatively 1¾ times the actual engine room tonnage.

The overall limit to the propelling power allowance for all ships, excluding tugs, is that the deduction is not to exceed 55 per cent of that part of the tonnage which remains after deducting from the gross tonnage the deductions allowed by Section 79 of the Merchant Shipping Act. Figure 49 shows graphically the British allowances for propelling power.

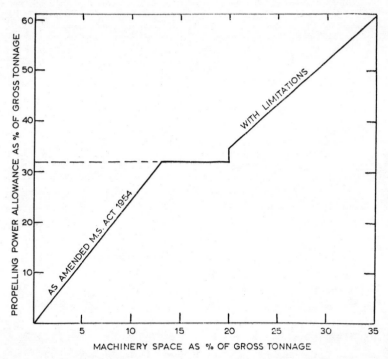

49 Propelling power allowance

(b) *Items under section 79 of the MSA*
These must be included in the gross tonnage before being deducted. The spaces include:

(1) Master's and crew accommodation
(2) Steering, anchor and capstan spaces if below the upper deck
(3) Chart room, lamp room and wireless room
(4) Boatswain's store subject to certain restrictions
(5) Donkey engine and boiler space if within the engine room
(6) Water ballast spaces other than double bottom.

A summary calculation in round figures of the method adopted to assess British tonnage is given below; this shows in progressive steps the items included and deducted from the gross tonnage in order to obtain the net tonnage.

EXAMPLE

Under deck	$=3685$	Propelling
Erections	$= 680$	power spaces $=530$.
Houses	$= 158$	

$$\frac{530}{4710}=11\cdot2 \text{ per cent}$$

4523 (under Under deck column total)

light and air $=120$

$$\frac{530+120}{4710+120}=\frac{650}{4830}=13\cdot5 \text{ per cent}$$

Excess of hatchways $= 187$		for maximum deduction include
4710		light and air

Hatchways $=210$
½ per cent of $4523= \underline{23}$
187

Light and air	$= 120$	
	4830	

Propelling power allowance
(PPA)$=32$ per cent of 4830
$=1546$ tons

Deductions under Section 79 of MSA
Crew spaces	$= 330$
Master and navigation spaces	$= 65$
Boatswain's stores 56 (1 per cent limit)$=$	48
Fore peak (water ballast)	$= 115$
	558

P.P.A. $=1546$
2104

Gross = 4830 tons
deduct 2104
Net 2726 tons

Suez and Panama Canal regulations

As stated earlier in this chapter, details of British Tonnage Rules are given in the publication *Instructions as to the Tonnage Measurement of Ships*, published by the Stationery Office. This contains information about Suez Canal Special Tonnage Certificates. The Panama Canal Tonnage is dealt with in a supplement.

Suez Canal Tonnage

The regulations for the Suez Canal Tonnage are rather similar to the British with small variations regarding exemptions and deductions. One very important point is that to gain the exemptions under Suez Rules the spaces concerned must also be entitled to exemption under British Rules. The forecastle is exempt for only one-eighth of the length of the ship from the inside of the stem, and the poop for one-tenth of the length from intersection of inside of frames. Within the open bridge space the only exemptions are for the space abreast the machinery space openings, and in way of permanent side openings. Light and air spaces are only exempt above first-tier erections.

The principal difference between the Suez and the British regulations is in the propelling power allowance (PPA). The Suez rules do not permit the 32 per cent deduction, but only $1\frac{3}{4}$ times the actual machinery space measurement. There is a limit to the PPA of 50 per cent of the gross tonnage which does not apply to tugs. The total deduction, apart from the PPA, may not exceed 10 per cent of the gross tonnage. Suez Canal Rules give, broadly, a tonnage value approximately that of the British Rules and somewhat greater than Panama.

Panama Canal Tonnage

The Panama rules were extensively revised in 1938 which resulted in a small reduction in the net tonnage of ordinary general cargo ships and a large reduction for passenger vessels. For the latter all public rooms, toilets and passages serving them became deductible items. Under the revised rules double bottom spaces not used for cargo became exempt.

The assessment of the machinery space is more exacting than the British rules as galleries and flats are excluded from the main engine room measurement if they contain service tanks, spares or stores taking up more than 50 per cent of the space of such parts. Settling tanks are also excluded. The limit in PPA is 50 per cent of the gross tonnage as is the case in the Suez rules.

IMCO

There is much international interest in tonnage measurement and considerable time has been devoted to it by the Inter-Governmental Maritime Consultative Organisation—IMCO—a United Nations agency, whose objective is to facilitate co-operation among governments on safety at sea, and in technical matters affecting shipping. IMCO has made a recommendation to governments regarding the treatment of 'shelter-deck' ships. Such ships have 'tonnage openings' in the topmost deck and the space below that deck and the next is included or excluded from the ship's tonnage according to the means of closing the opening.

Most countries agree that 'tonnage openings' serve no useful purpose and indeed some countries consider such openings unsafe.

The new system is the tonnage mark system and abolishes the temporary means of closing openings in bulkheads and deck as a condition for exemption from tonnage of the spaces to which the openings give access. Consequently, the open shelter deck ship will disappear and with it the open shelter deck/closed shelter deck (OSD/CSD) convertible type. The two deck ship of the future, when designed for maximum deadweight, will have two tonnages but only one freeboard assigned; the greater tonnage will include all spaces below the weather deck, which will also be the deck from which the freeboard will be assigned; the smaller tonnage will include all spaces below the second deck only, the 'tween deck spaces being exempt even although they are without tonnage openings. A new special tonnage mark, to be set off from the second deck, will be assigned by the Tonnage Authority and will be cut in on the ship's sides. Provided this special tonnage mark is not submerged the smaller tonnage will be that of the ship; if it is submerged, the greater tonnage will apply. This means that draught will control tonnage directly.

If the two deck ship of the future is designed for minimum tonnage and not for maximum tonnage it will have one tonnage and one freeboard. The owners of current open shelter deckers who desire to retain the OSD tonnage and draught when the tonnage mark system comes into operation can have the freeboard calculated from the second deck and the new special tonnage mark placed at the load-line level.

Details of the tonnage mark system and the new special tonnage mark are given below. Most maritime countries were invited by IMCO to give effect to the tonnage mark system. No specific date has been fixed, nor other conditions made, for its coming into force. The system will thus become effective for each country independent of others.

The trend in tonnage measurement is towards a universal system, to be followed by a simplified system. Such a system should have rules

(1) That are fair between those who provide shipping services and those who pay for them

(2) That are fair between one ship and another

(3) That do not have a fundamental bearing on ship design

(4) That are capable of simple application

The recommendations on the 'Treatment of Shelter-Deck and other Open Spaces' are reproduced below from the IMCO publication and with IMCO's permission.

General

(1) Pending the establishment of a universal system of tonnage measurement provisions should be introduced into the present national tonnage measurement requirements so that those spaces of a permanent character which are regarded as open spaces and are accordingly exempted from inclusion in gross tonnage under

such rules, may be permanently closed, while retaining the present exemption of those spaces.

(2) More specifically, such provisions should extend to all ships and should permit exemption from gross tonnage of:

(a) certain permanently closed spaces situated on or above the uppermost complete deck exposed to sea and weather; and

(b) certain permanently closed spaces situated between the above mentioned uppermost complete deck and the complete deck next below [i.e. the second deck], provided that a tonnage mark as hereinafter defined is not submerged.

Tonnage mark

(3) TONNAGE MARK REFERENCE DECK. The tonnage mark should be located at a certain distance below the line of the second deck, the position of such line being as defined for a deck-line in the International Load Line Convention in force.

(4) LOCATION OF TONNAGE MARK. The distance referred to in Paragraph 3 above should be calculated by using the tonnage mark table—see later.

The tonnage mark and the statutory load-line

(5) The tonnage mark, see Figure 51, should be marked on each side of the ship slightly abaft amidships, i.e. sufficiently away from the statutory load-line mark to avoid confusion between the two marks. In no case should the tonnage mark be assigned above the appropriate statutory load-line. Nothing in these recommendations would prevent the assignment of a statutory load-line on the assumption that the second deck is the freeboard deck. When the statutory load-line is so assigned, the tonnage mark may be placed at the same level, without regard to any tabular assignment which would otherwise be required.

Use of tonnage mark in determining tonnage

(6) When the tonnage mark is *not* submerged, the gross and net tonnages determined by *exempting* the spaces which qualify for

exemption in accordance with Paragraph 8 below and which are situated within the uppermost 'tween deck should apply; when the tonnage mark *is* submerged, the gross and net tonnages determined *without* exempting the said spaces should be applicable.

Detached superstructures and deck-houses

(7) The spaces which qualify for exemption and which are situated in the detached superstructures or deck-houses on or above the uppermost complete deck, should be exempt from inclusion in the gross tonnage, whether or not the tonnage mark is submerged.

Spaces qualifying for exemption

(8) Those spaces which are permanently closed but which, were they provided with tonnage openings, would be exempt from inclusion in the gross tonnage under the present relevant national tonnage measurement requirements, should qualify for exemption, provided that:

(*a*) if the above spaces are situated on or above the uppermost complete deck, they should be *exempt* from inclusion in the gross tonnage *irrespective* of the draught (Paragraph 7);

(*b*) if the spaces are situated within the uppermost 'tween deck; and

   (*i*) if the tonnage mark is *not* submerged, the spaces should be *exempt* from inclusion in the gross tonnage;

   (*ii*) if, on the other hand, the tonnage mark *is* submerged, the spaces should be *included* in the gross tonnage (Paragraph 6).

Entry in the tonnage certificate of information on the spaces exempted

(9) Pertinent information on the spaces which have been exempted from inclusion in the gross tonnage in accordance with Paragraphs 8(*a*) and 8(*b*)(*i*) should be entered in the tonnage certificate, in a manner similar to the present practice in regard to the spaces not included in the gross tonnage.

Control of tonnage

(10) TONNAGE CERTIFICATE. If a ship has a tonnage mark, the tonnage certificate of the ship should show two sets of gross and net tonnages determined in accordance with Paragraph 8 above, except that when the statutory load-line is assigned on the assumption that the second deck is the freeboard deck and the tonnage mark is placed at the same level as the load-line mark, only one set of tonnages need be shown. (The term 'tonnage certificate' also covers the 'certificate of registry'.)

Validation of applicable tonnage

(11) The applicable set of tonnages should be determined either (a) in accordance with the ship's loading condition, i.e. whether the tonnage mark is submerged or not, or (b) by the validation by the national authorities concerned of either of the two sets of tonnages for a certain period or for the voyage, as appropriate.

Uses of dual tonnages

(12) When the tonnage certificate shows two sets of tonnages the higher set of tonnages will apply for the purposes of safety. Apart from this safety consideration, the choice between the two sets of tonnages for any particular purpose is left to the interests concerned.

Application

(13) The above provisions should be applicable to all ships, whether existing or new.

Relationship to any universal system of tonnage measurement

(14) The above provisions should not necessarily form an integral part of any universal system of tonnage measurement.

Exchange of information between governments

(15) Governments should exchange, through the organisation, relevant information as to their practices in the matters covered by these recommendations, the object being to ensure international uniformity as far as practicable in the interpretation and application of the recommendations.

Definitions

(1) The UPPERMOST COMPLETE DECK exposed to sea and weather, as referred to in Paragraph 2 of the above recommendations, shall be the deck which has permanent means of closing all openings in the weather portions thereof, provided that all openings in the sides of the ship below that deck are fitted with permanent means of watertight closing, other than any openings situated abaft a transverse watertight bulkhead placed aft of the rudder stock.

(2) The SECOND DECK shall be the deck next below the uppermost complete deck which is continuous in a fore and aft direction at least between peak bulkheads, is continuous athwartships, and is fitted as an integral and permanent part of the vessel's structure, with proper covers fitted to all main hatchways. Interruptions in way of propelling machinery space openings, ladder and stairway openings, trunks, chain lockers, cofferdams or steps not exceeding a total height of 48 in shall not be deemed to break the continuity of the deck.

The term 'trunks' as used in this definition is intended to mean hatch and ventilation trunks which do not extend longitudinally completely between main transverse bulkheads.

(3) The LENGTH (L_t) used in the tonnage mark table shall be the distance on the second deck between two points, of which the foremost is the point where the underside of that deck or the line thereof at the stem, meets the inner surface of the ceiling, sparring or frames, and the aftermost is the point where the underside of that deck, or the line thereof, meets the inner surface of the ceiling, sparring or frames in the middle plane at the stern. Where the

second deck is stepped an equivalent length shall be used (Figure 50).

(4) The DEPTH (D_s) to be used in the tonnage mark table is the

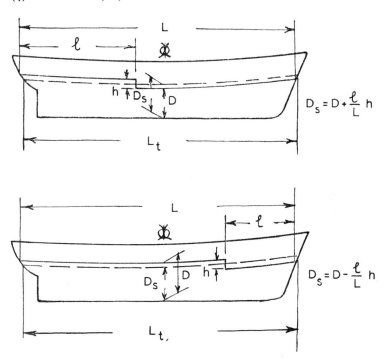

$$D_s = D + \frac{\ell}{L} h$$

$$D_s = D - \frac{\ell}{L} h$$

50 Length and depth of tonnage mark table

moulded depth to the second deck. Where the second deck is stepped an equivalent depth shall be used (Figure 50).

Tonnage mark table

(5) The tonnage mark table is given below. The figures in the table are the minimum distances from the moulded line of the second deck or, where the second deck is stepped, from the equivalent thereof, to the upper edge of the tonnage mark.

(6) The tonnage mark table is given for the ratios L_t/D_s from 12 to 20, where L_t and D_s are the length and depth as defined above.

(7) The tonnage mark table is presented for lengths up to 800 ft at intervals of 10 ft.

(8) For intermediate lengths and L_t/D_s ratios the corresponding distance should be obtained by linear interpolation. For other cases figures may be obtained by extrapolation.

Form of the tonnage mark

(9) The tonnage mark shall consist of a horizontal line 15 in long and 1 in wide, upon which shall be placed for identification an inverted equilateral triangle, each side 12 in long and 1 in wide, with its apex on the mid-point of this line (Figure 51).

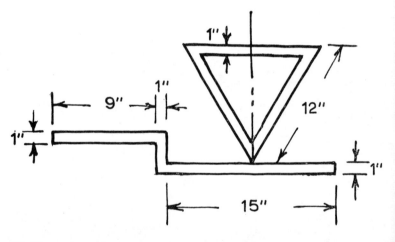

51 Tonnage mark

The upper edge of the horizontal line indicates the maximum draught to which the ship can be loaded if the exemption of certain spaces in the uppermost 'tween deck is to be maintained.

(10) An additional line indicating similarly permissible draught for fresh water and in tropical waters may be assigned.

Tonnage mark table
Minimum distance (in inches) from the moulded line of the second deck to the upper edge of the tonnage mark

$\dfrac{Lt}{Ds}$ / Length L_t in ft	12	13	14	15	16	17	18	19	20
220 and under	2·0	2·0	2·0	2·0	2·0	2·0	2·0	2·0	2·0
230	3·2	2·0	2·0	2·0	2·0	2·0	2·0	2·0	2·0
240	4·7	2·0	2·0	2·0	2·0	2·0	2·0	2·0	2·0
250	6·3	3·3	2·0	2·0	2·0	2·0	2·0	2·0	2·0
260	8·0	4·8	2·1	2·0	2·0	2·0	2·0	2·0	2·0
270	9·9	6·4	3·5	2·0	2·0	2·0	2·0	2·0	2·0
280	11·8	8·1	4·9	2·1	2·0	2·0	2·0	2·0	2·0
290	13·9	9·9	6·5	3·5	2·0	2·0	2·0	2·0	2·0
300	16·0	11·7	8·1	4·9	2·1	2·0	2·0	2·0	2·0
310	18·3	13·7	9·8	6·4	3·5	2·0	2·0	2·0	2·0
320	20·7	15·8	11·7	8·1	4·9	2·1	2·0	2·0	2·0
330	23·2	18·0	13·6	9·8	6·4	3·5	2·0	2·0	2·0
340	25·9	20·4	15·7	11·6	8·1	4·9	2·1	2·0	2·0
350	28·7	22·9	17·9	13·6	9·8	6·5	3·6	2·0	2·0
360	31·7	25·5	20·2	15·7	11·7	8·2	5·0	2·2	2·0
370	34·7	28·3	22·7	17·9	13·6	9·9	6·6	3·7	2·0
380	38·0	31·1	25·3	20·2	15·7	11·8	8·3	5·2	2·4
390	41·3	34·1	27·9	22·6	17·9	13·8	10·1	6·8	3·8
400	44·8	37·2	30·7	25·0	20·1	15·8	11·9	8·4	5·3
410	48·2	40·3	33·5	27·7	22·6	18·1	14·0	10·4	7·2
420	51·5	43·4	36·4	30·4	25·2	20·6	16·4	12·7	9·4
430	54·8	46·5	39·4	33·3	27·9	23·2	19·0	15·2	11·8
440	58·4	49·9	42·6	36·4	30·9	26·0	21·7	17·8	14·4
450	62·1	53·4	46·0	39·6	33·9	29·0	24·6	20·6	17·1
460	65·9	57·0	49·5	42·9	37·1	32·1	27·6	23·5	19·9
470	69·8	60·7	53·0	46·3	40·4	35·2	30·6	26·5	22·8
480	73·7	64·4	56·5	49·7	43·7	38·4	33·7	29·5	25·7
490	77·5	68·1	60·0	53·0	46·9	41·5	36·7	32·4	28·5
500	81·2	71·6	63·4	56·2	50·0	44·5	39·6	35·2	31·2
510	84·9	75·1	66·7	59·4	53·0	47·4	42·4	37·9	33·9
520	88·4	78·4	69·9	62·4	55·9	50·2	45·1	40·5	36·4
530	91·8	81·6	72·9	65·3	58·7	52·9	47·7	43·0	38·8
540	95·2	84·8	75·9	68·1	61·4	55·5	50·2	45·4	41·2
550	98·4	87·8	78·8	70·9	64·0	58·0	52·6	47·8	43·4
560	101·6	90·8	81·6	73·6	66·6	60·5	55·0	50·1	45·6
570	104·8	93·8	84·4	76·3	69·2	62·9	57·3	52·3	47·8
580	107·9	96·8	87·2	78·9	71·7	65·3	59·6	54·5	49·9
590	111·0	99·7	90·0	81·5	74·2	67·7	61·9	56·7	52·0
600	114·0	102·5	92·6	84·0	76·5	69·9	64·0	58·8	54·0
610	117·0	105·3	95·2	86·5	78·9	72·1	66·2	60·8	56·0

Tonnage mark table (continued

$\dfrac{Lt}{Ds}$									
Length L_t in ft	12	13	14	15	16	17	18	19	20
620	120·0	108·0	97·8	88·9	81·2	74·4	68·3	62·8	58·0
630	122·9	110·7	100·4	91·3	83·5	76·6	70·4	64·8	59·9
640	125·7	113·4	102·9	93·7	85·8	78·7	72·4	66·8	61·7
650	128·6	116·1	105·4	96·1	88·0	80·8	74·4	68·7	63·6
660	131·4	118·7	107·8	98·3	90·1	82·8	76·3	70·6	65·3
670	134·2	121·2	110·2	110·6	92·2	84·8	78·3	72·4	67·1
680	136·9	123·8	112·6	102·9	94·3	86·8	80·2	74·2	68·9
690	139·6	126·3	115·0	105·1	96·4	88·8	82·1	76·0	70·6
700	142·3	128·8	117·3	107·3	98·5	90·8	83·9	77·8	72·3
710	144·9	131·3	119·6	109·4	100·5	92·7	85·7	79·5	73·9
720	147·5	133·7	121·8	111·5	102·5	94·6	87·5	81·2	75·5
730	150·1	136·1	124·0	113·6	104·5	96·5	89·3	82·9	77·1
740	152·7	138·5	126·2	115·7	106·5	98·3	91·1	84·5	78·7
750	155·3	140·8	128·5	117·8	108·4	100·1	92·8	86·1	80·3
760	157·8	143·1	130·6	119·7	110·3	101·9	94·4	87·8	81·7
770	160·2	145·4	132·7	121·7	112·1	103·6	96·0	89·3	83·2
780	162·6	147·6	134·8	123·7	113·9	105·3	97·6	90·8	84·7
790	165·1	149·9	136·9	125·6	115·7	107·0	99·2	92·3	86·1
800	167·5	152·1	138·9	127·4	117·4	108·6	100·8	93·8	87·4

The allowance to be used in fixing this additional line shall be $\frac{1}{48}$ of the moulded draught to the tonnage mark.

(11) The additional line shall be a horizontal line 9 in long and 1 in wide, measured from a vertical line, the latter 1 in wide, being marked at the after end of, and perpendicular to, the tonnage mark (Figure 51).

(12) When, in accordance with Paragraph 5 of the Recommendations, the tonnage mark is placed at the same level as the appropriate statutory load-line, it may be marked on a line level with the uppermost part of the load-line grid, in which case the additional line for fresh water and tropical waters shall not be used.

Longitudinal position of the tonnage mark

(13) The tonnage mark shall be placed abaft amidships but as

near thereto as practicable, and in no case shall the apex of the triangle be nearer than 21 in to the centre of the load-line disc nor farther than 6 ft 6 in abaft the vertical centre line of the load-line disc.

Other matters

(14) No line of the second deck shall be marked.

(15) For ships having no statutory load-line, the line of the uppermost complete deck shall be marked similarly to the deck-line in the Load-Line Convention.

(16) The tonnage certificate shall show the vertical distance from the upper edge of the deck-line to the upper edge of the tonnage mark.

Freeboard

The maximum waterline to which a ship can be loaded is controlled by the freeboard marks which are permanently marked on the ship's sides at the middle of the length. Freeboard is the amount of the side of the ship out of the water. The minimum freeboard is the height amidships of the freeboard deck at side above the normal summer load-line.

The fundamental reason for statutory enforcement of a limiting load-line was to protect seamen against the risk of proceeding to sea in unseaworthy ships. The history of the development of rules for the compulsory limitation of the draught of ships is of some interest. The study of this question is generally concentrated on the minimum freeboard rather than on the maximum draught.

In 1835 the Committee of Lloyd's Register of Shipping proposed that a freeboard of 3 in per ft depth of hold should be taken as a guide to safe loading. The Liverpool Underwriters, about the same time made an attempt to regulate the loading of ships and suggested a freeboard per foot depth of hold which varied with the depth—from $2\frac{1}{4}$ in per ft in small ships to 4 in per ft in larger ships. In 1867 the Institution of Naval Architects made certain

L

recommendations to the Board of Trade concerning freeboard and in 1871 a Merchant Shipping Act was passed making provision for the marking of a scale of feet showing the draught of water at the stem and the stern. By this Act the Board of Trade were empowered to record the draughts on seagoing ships when they left port.

It was during this period that Samuel Plimsoll, whose name will always be associated with the subject of freeboard, made a successful fight in Parliament for the marking of all ships with a line indicating the limit to which they could be loaded. A number of Acts were passed and by 1876 it was compulsory for the deck line to be marked and the owner was required to mark a disc on the sides of the ship showing the maximum draught to which he proposed to load. This disc was popularly known as the Plimsoll mark. However, although the marking of a maximum load-line was compulsory its position was left to the discretion of the owner.

Over the years several suggestions about freeboard were made and in 1883 a Committee was appointed by the President of the Board of Trade to consider general rules concerning freeboard and the feasibility of freeboard tables. Their recommendations with the submitted freeboard tables were accepted by the Board of Trade in 1886 but there was no legal obligation for their assignment and were only marked on the voluntary application of the owner. However, this was changed by the Merchant Shipping Act of 1890 which required all British ships, except fishing vessels, yachts, etc., to have freeboards assigned in accordance with the tables and regulations. The basic requirements of the Act were in operation until a major revision was made in 1906. These remained operative until 1930.

The first International Conference on Load Lines was held in London in 1930 at the invitation of the United Kingdom Government. The resulting agreement, the 1930 Load Line Convention, codified for the first time rules which would be internationally applicable.

The underlying principles of the freeboard regulations are:
(a) The ship must be structurally efficient.
Ships which comply with the highest standard of the rules of an

approved Classification Society are regarded as having sufficient strength.

(b) The freeboard assigned is such that when the ship is loaded to the marks there is sufficient reserve buoyancy in the hull above the waterline to ensure a satisfactory margin of safety. By reserve buoyancy is meant that portion of the ship above the waterline which is intact.

The years subsequent to 1930 brought about great changes in ship design and construction; welding, new types of closing appliances such as metal hatch covers made a great improvement in ensuring a ship's watertight integrity; ships increased in length, particularly tankers—the 1930 Convention only covered tankers up to 600 ft in length. These factors indicated that there was need for new and up-to-date regulations. In 1959 a meeting of Classification Societies advocated the need for new load-line regulations. In that year IMCO—Inter-Governmental Maritime Consultative Organisation—had just come into being and was entrusted with the task of preparing the new convention.

The second International Conference on Load Lines ended on 5th April 1966, with the signature of an agreement—the International Convention on Load Lines 1966. This convention will come into force 12 months after it has been accepted by at least 15 countries, seven of which possess not less than 1,000,000 tons gross of shipping. It is of interest to consider briefly the effects of the new Convention. As compared with its predecessor, the new Convention introduces a number of changes, the most significant of which is the reduction in freeboards for large ships. Large tankers, ore carriers, and bulk carriers will have their freeboards reduced by about 10 to 20 per cent; dry cargo ships if fitted with weathertight hatch covers will also benefit by a reduction of up to 10 per cent approximately. The freeboard of small ships will be slightly increased in order to improve stability. This increase of up to 2 in will only apply to new ships fitted with wooden hatch covers and tarpaulins. This will encourage the adoption of steel hatch covers. Existing ships with metal hatch covers will not be affected. The new freeboard tables cover ships up to 1200 ft in length.

Another important improvement in the safety of ships is the

complete elimination of the provisions for Class 2 closing appliances and tonnage openings; this means that only superstructures fitted with gasketed weathertight doors will be taken into account in freeboard computation.

Fishing vessels are not covered by the 1966 Convention. The conference established criteria for estimating weather conditions and these criteria were used as a basis when constituting the zones, areas and seasonal periods. The boundaries of the winter seasonal zones were changed considerably, particularly in the North Atlantic and the South Pacific.

Such, in brief, are the main changes embodied in the 1966 Load Line Convention, which comes into force on July 21, 1968.

Reference is made in Appendix I to the important features of the Convention Regulations.

VII · MERCHANT SHIP REGISTRATION: LAUNCHING: SPEED TRIALS

The first British Merchant Shipping Act and the appointment of surveyors to the Marine Department of the Board of Trade was passed in 1854.

Registration

The registration of British ships was made compulsory by the Navigation Acts of 1660 and onwards. The British Registry Act of 1786 made it compulsory for every ship to have the name of the vessel and the port to which she belonged painted on the stern and the certificate of registration had to contain details of dimensions.

Under the terms of the Merchant Shipping Act of 1894 every British ship, with certain minor exemptions, must be registered. A vessel coming within the Act and not so registered is not considered a British ship. The ship's master must always have the certificate of registry—termed the ship's register—in his possession on board; in default of this the ship is liable to be detained.

Before registration the ship must be surveyed by a Board of Trade surveyor and measured for tonnage in accordance with the regulations. The official completes a form giving details of tonnages, displacement, propelling machinery and a certification of the draught marks. For the latter the surveyor inspects and checks the draught marks which are cut in on each side of the stem and sternpost either in Roman capital letters of figures, not less than 6 in in height and painted white or yellow on a dark ground. The completed form together with certain particulars of the crew spaces are forwarded to the Register of Shipping.

Application for registry must be made by the owner of the ship, and such application accompanied by a special declaration of ownership. For the first registry of a new ship, a builders' certificate, giving details of where the ship was built, tonnages, etc., must also be submitted to the Registrar.

When all the necessary documents are available to the Registrar, the required particulars are entered in the Official Register Book under the next available number, and eventually a Certificate of Registry is prepared for the ship. This certificate is essential in connection with most of the ship's business and movements. Prior to the actual delivery of this certificate, a 'carving note' is issued by the Registrar giving details of the required markings on and in the ship; these are:

(a) The ship's name to be marked on each side of the bow and the name and port of registry on the stern in letters not less than 4 in in height.

(b) The official number and net tonnage to be marked on a main beam.

The satisfactory marking of these particulars is certified by the Board of Trade Surveyor on the carving note and the Certificate of Registry can then be issued by the Registrar in exchange for the duly signed carving note.

The Merchant Shipping Act of 1894 and those that followed stipulate:

(1) That the property in a ship shall be divided into sixty-four shares.

(2) That not more than sixty-four individuals shall be entitled to be registered at the same time as owners of any one ship.

(3) That a person shall not be entitled to be registered as owner of a fractional part of a share in a ship, but any number of persons not exceeding five may be registered as joint owners of a ship or of any share or shares therein.

Naming ships

The control of naming ships dates from 1696 when the Navigation Acts relating to the registration of merchant ships were consolidated. The law was brought into being in order to combat frauds and regulate abuses in the plantation trade. At that time the law provided that only certain ships should be registered but a new Act in 1786 made registration compulsory for all ships, with a few exceptions. The current law is based on the Merchant Shipping Acts of 1894 and 1906. If another ship already bears the proposed name, permission may be refused for the vessel to be registered under that name. An exception may be made in special circumstances, such as when the new ship is to replace an old ship of the same name. It is of interest to note that the Clyde pleasure steamer *Queen Mary* was renamed *Queen Mary II*.

A ship may have the name and port of registry changed in certain regulated circumstances, but the official number allotted to a ship on first registry is never changed. If a ship ceases to be a British ship by reason of sale or other circumstances, the vessel's Register Book must be returned to the Registrar at the appropriate port of registry, and the registration is duly cancelled. If this vessel again comes into British ownership, the ship must be re-registered after survey and will be allotted the original official number.

Ship names

For many years Japanese merchant ships have carried the suffix 'Maru' in their names. It was not known with certainty how the word originated as far as ships are concerned but it has been suggested that it came from a castle on land and that the superstructure of a ship reminded people of such a building. The Japan Line has decided to dispense with the word in their future ships. The company explains that as Japanese names are difficult for foreigners to understand and remember, this disadvantage is to be overcome by using English names. Their ships in future will have the prefix 'Japan'. For the identification of type it is intended to use the names of flowers for tankers and names of trees for dry cargo ships. The initial step in this new method of naming was to invite shareholders to submit names for two new tankers and two new dry cargo ships. The names selected for the tankers were: *Japan Lily*; *Japan Rose*; and for the dry cargo ships: *Japan Pine*; *Japan Elm*.

Launching ceremonies

The ceremony of breaking a bottle of wine over the bows of a ship is supposed to have had its origin in the superstition that all great ventures could only be successful if at their initiation they were accompanied by the shedding of human blood. The burnt sacrifices of the ancients, when slaves or prisoners of war were killed, and in later days the substitution of animals for human beings, are all instances of the practice of this superstition, and it has been recorded that explorers have found that savages launch their war canoes over the bodies of human beings, an obvious example of the practice of the same superstitious rite. Today in this country, and in the majority of maritime countries, at all launching ceremonies wine forms an agreeable substitute for blood.

The operation of the Prohibition Acts in the USA—during what was considered by many people as a misguided period in American history—robbed the time-honoured ceremony of christening a ship of much of its traditional meaning, and sailor-men pointed out that all kinds of unfortunate accidents had occurred when Father Neptune was insulted with inferior liquid. Among these were the launch of HMS *Albion* on the Thames in 1898. On this occasion the principles of one of the leading men in the ship-building world were respected and the champagne was replaced by water. As camouflage the bottle was swathed with ribbons, forming quite an effective pad, and the then Duchess of York had to throw it three times before she could break it. Within a few moments about forty spectators had been drowned by the back-wash of the launch carrying away a stage. The American tanker *Bidwell* stuck half-way down the ways after she had been christened with ginger ale. More attention was directed to these incidents than the occasions merited, but sailors are a superstitious class. At the launch of one American ship the crowning indignity was perpetrated by sending the ship on its way with a baptism of ice-cream.

A vessel for the Indian coastal trade, built in this country, had a launching ceremony which was unusual and picturesque. The naming ceremony was preceded by a religious service and instead of the customary bottle of wine, a coconut was used in the naming ceremony, the ship itself, as well as a number of the guests, being garlanded with flowers. At the launch of a ship, also in this country, for Chinese owners, the Chinese national flag was unfurled, which the launching company saluted. As the vessel moved down the ways a number of crackers and other fireworks were exploded. This is an ancient Chinese custom and is done by way of jubilation to wish prosperity and peace for the new ship.

With ships for the Royal Navy the launching ceremony may be taken as standardised, the only change in over a hundred years being the provision of a safety lashing, generally a riband, since one excited royal lady acting as sponsor to a ship missed the bow completely and laid out a spectator with the bottle of champagne.

One of the Clyde's strangest launchings took place in December 1966 when a frigate ordered by the Ghana Government before the overthrow of the Nkrumah regime, was launched without a name. The builders' chairman said that there would be no crowds of workers present. At the time of the launch it was not known if Ghana still wanted the warship.

Many speeches have been made at the launching of ships and frequently the opportunity is taken to review the position of the shipbuilding and shipping industries. The speech made by the Queen at the launching of the Cunarder which bore her name is worth recalling. The following is an extract:

'We do not forget the men who brought this great ship into being. For them she must ever be a source of pride, and I am sure of affection. I congratulate them warmly on the fruits of their labour. The launch of a ship is like the inception of all great human enterprises—an act of faith. We cannot foretell the future, but in preparing for it we show our trust in a divine providence and in ourselves.'

The shipbuilding industry for generations has been a feast—or—famine affair. The ordering of a ship for some twenty years of trading is at any time an act of faith and courage.

When one considers the thousands of ships that have been

launched even in the last century, the freedom from accident, serious or otherwise, is really remarkable. On the Clyde in 1883 the *Daphne*, after launching, capsized with heavy loss of life. This accident brought about regulations regarding the number of men on board during a launch. It also showed the necessity for calculating the stability under launching conditions. The Italian liner *Principessa Jolanda* capsized after being launched from the shipyard near Genoa in 1907. This vessel sank in a quarter of an hour, became buried in the sand, and was finally a total loss. She was launched with machinery on board and apparently without sufficient ballast. In 1908 the steamer *Patris*, built on the Tyne, broke the drag ropes and careered across the river into a dry dock which contained another ship. The *Bismarck*, launched at Hamburg in 1939, ran aground, and in spite of the efforts of tugs, it took some hours before she could be towed to the fitting-out berth. A remarkable launch was that of the aircraft carrier *Formidable* when launched at Belfast, the forward cradle was actually left behind as the vessel continued her course down the ways.

The history of launching is rather obscure, and although bow-first launching was widely practised in the eighteenth century, present-day practice almost universally favours stern-first launching, except for a small amount of broadside launching into narrow waterways.

The foregoing on launching ceremonies is part of an article on 'The Launching of Ships' contributed by the author to the *Shipbuilding and Shipping Record*, and is given here by permission of the editor of that journal.

Launching: general considerations

The launching of a great ship is a most spectacular engineering feat and a large amount of work has to be done prior to this one short period of tremendous dynamic action. The transference of a ship-weighing, for a cargo vessel, about 3,000 tons, to one of the Cunarder Queens of about 36,700 tons—to the water from the building berth is an operation involving the risk of serious damage to the ship. It is thus necessary to have some knowledge of the forces brought into action during the process of launching before the operation is commenced.

The invariable practice in this country is to launch the ship down two 'ways', placed parallel to the centre line of the ship and about one-third of the ship's breadth apart. These ways are known as the groundways and consist of long baulks of timber laid on top of a series of blocks; the ways slope downward to the water. The sliding ways on which the ship is carried to the water usually extend under the ship for about 80 per cent of the length. They consist also of long baulks of timber and are surmounted by a cradle by which the weight of the ship is transferred to them. The end portions of the cradle are commonly known as the poppets. A thick grease is applied between the sliding and ground ways at a late stage in the erection of the launching arrangements.

When the ship and cradle are sliding down the ways and before the ship is completely afloat there are three critical positions.

(1) When the centre of gravity (G) of the ship has passed over the after end of the ground ways (AEGW) the tendency of the ship may be to turn about the AEGW and so concentrate a load at that point. Such a load may be beyond the capacity of the ends of the ground ways and they may collapse.

(2) When the buoyancy aft is sufficient to lift the ship and tend to turn the vessel about the fore end of the cradle and thereby exert a great pressure in that region.

(3) When the cradle leaves the ways and the fore end of the ship drops off the end of the ways, it is essential to ensure that the immersion will not be so great as to cause the forefoot to strike the ground below the AEGW.

These three positions are indicated in Figure 52

The details of launchway construction and the calculations involved investigating the critical positions enumerated above are rather outside the scope of this book.

Speed and power trials

Almost invariably in every ship contract a speed is specified which the ship must be able to attain. Consequently when the ship is completed speed trials are run to ascertain:

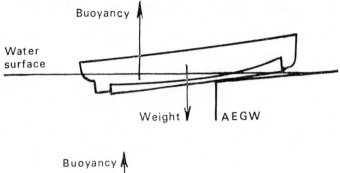

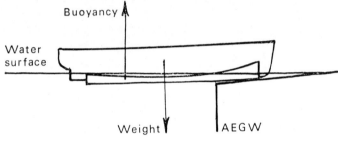

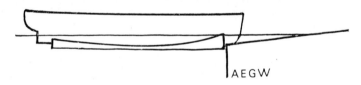

52 Launching

(1) that contract requirements with regard to speed, power and fuel consumption have been attained.

(2) full-scale data on the performance of the ship that can be used in future estimates of power, speed and performance.

There are two types of speed trials:

(1) A trial at a single speed to satisfy contract requirements.

(2) A progressive speed trial where the ship is run at a series of speeds from a low speed working up to the maximum that can be reached.

The specified trial speed is generally greater than the expected service speed since the trial will be run under smooth water conditions and thus for a given power a greater speed should be possible than in service. Moreover the trial is generally conducted at a displacement less than the fully loaded condition.

Measured-mile trials

There are several ways in which speed can be measured but the most satisfactory method for speed trials is to run the ship on a measured mile course. The layout of such a course is shown in Figure 53. Two pairs of posts, AB and CD, are erected on land and of sufficient height to be visible when some distance out at sea. The lines AB and CD are parallel to one another and one nautical mile (6080 ft) apart and the ship's course is steered at right-angles to these lines. The time interval between the ship being abreast the line AB and being abreast the line CD will be the time taken to cover one nautical mile. This time divided into one hour gives the speed of the ship in knots relative to the land. On trial the posts are sighted by means of binoculars and the instant the two posts come into line with the ship can be ascertained. Time is measured by means of a stop watch. To eliminate the effect of tide, several runs are taken both with and against the tide.

To ensure accuracy in the determination of the ship's speed from the observed times of successive runs over a measured mile course the following should be noted:

(a) the successive runs should be made in opposite directions over the same course.

(b) On completing a run the ship should be immediately turned off the course under a small angle of helm and run a sufficient distance before the turn so as to give a straight run prior to re-entering the mile course. This is shown in Figure 53.

(c) The time intervals between the runs on the mile should be about equal and as short as possible.

(d) The mean speed (V) and mean revolutions per minute should be determined by the mean of means method or from the averaging formula given below.

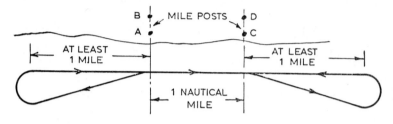

53 Measured mile

Assume four speeds obtained were V_1 V_2 V_3 and V_4 the true speed (V) of the ship through the water is given by

$$V = \frac{V_1 + 3V_2 + 3V_3 + V_4}{8}$$

The measured mile trial should be run as far as possible in fine weather when there is little or no wind. Should there be a high wind blowing when the ship is on the mile the air resistance will be increased and it is then necessary to make a further correction to the observed speeds. It is usual to put the vessel in dry dock before going on trial so that the underwater portion of the ship can be cleaned and painted and in this way increase in resistance due to fouling can be avoided. It is desirable, where possible, to run the speed trials at the load displacement but for dry cargo ships it is often difficult to obtain the necessary deadweight for this to be done. This difficulty does not arise with tankers as the fully loaded draught can be obtained by filling the tanks with water ballast. The displacement of the ship at the trial must be accurately determined and this is done by noting the draughts and making use of the displacement data provided by the shipbuilder.

In addition to the measurement of speed during the trial the power and revolutions per minute of the propeller shaft are also obtained. There are several ways of measuring power and the method employed depends upon the type of machinery. The shaft horse power (SHP) on trial is determined by the twist of the shaft over a known length. This is done by an instrument known as a torsionmeter. The torsionmeter is capable of measuring the angle through which two selected points on the shaft twist relative to one

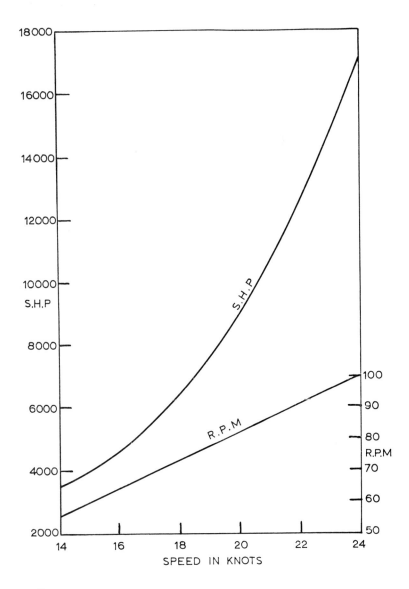

54 Power curve

another when the shaft is transmitting power. It is possible to obtain from the torsionmeter readings the torque being transmitted when the shaft is rotating and this in association with the revolutions per minute allows the shaft horse power delivered to the propeller to be calculated.

The trial data of power and revolutions per minute are plotted to a base of speed. The type of curves obtained are shown in Figure 54. In general the curve of revolutions to a base of speed is almost a straight line over a considerable range of speeds. The power curve shows a rapid increase with increase of speed. The ratio SHP÷speed^3 is often as in this case almost constant over a wide range of speed. This shows that the power is proportional to the speed.^{3}

VIII · MERCHANT SHIPPING ACT REGULATIONS

Statutory regulations are laid down by the Board of Trade, representing the British Government. The primary object of statutory regulations is to promote safety of life at sea, and the Board of Trade issues rules with which ships must comply. These rules are compulsory and are enforced by the various Merchant Shipping Acts. It is the purpose of the Government to ensure that the standards appropriate to safety are adopted. The international scope of the operations of ships has considerable bearing on the interrelation between the regulations of different governments. Comparable uniformity on an international scale has been made by means of Conferences, at which conventions were formulated. Illustrative of this are the International Load Line Convention and the International Convention for the Safety of Life at Sea.

Chapter IX deals with the means for saving the ship and those who travel in them in the event of an accident. A portion of this chapter is devoted to other ways in which the safety of the ship is secured and which have prevented accidents taking place.

Light and sound signals

International regulations for preventing collisions at sea require the provision of proper navigation lights and means of making

M

sound signals in all ships. The Rules concerning lights must be complied with in all weathers from sunset to sunrise and during such times no other lights can be exhibited, except such lights as cannot be mistaken for the prescribed lights or impair their visibility or distinctive character.

The Collision Regulations require that all power-driven vessels of 40 tons gross and over must be provided with one or two masthead lights according to the length of the vessel—vessels less than 150 ft in length are not required to carry a second light but may do so—two side lights, one stern light, two 'not-under-command' lights, and one or two anchor lights according to the length of the vessel.

The general disposition of these lights is shown in Figure 55.

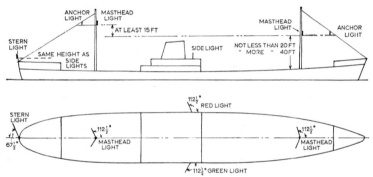

55 Navigation lights

Masthead lights

These two white lights are to be placed in a line with and over the keel so that the after light shall be at least 15 ft higher than the other. The lower light is to be not less than 20 ft above the hull and not more than 40 ft. The horizontal distance between the two white lights to be at least three times the vertical distance. The bright white light to be so constructed as to show an unbroken light over an arc of the horizon of 20 points of the compass (225 degrees) so fixed as to show 10 points ($112\frac{1}{2}$ degrees) on each side of the vessel. These lights must be visible at a distance of at least five miles.

Side lights

All vessels are fitted on the starboard side with a green light and on the port side with a red light. These lights so constructed as to show an unbroken light over an arc of the horizon of 10 points of the compass (112½ degrees) so fixed as to show the light from right ahead to 2 points (22½ degrees) abaft the beam. These lights must be visible at a distance of at least two miles. The lights are fitted with inboard screens projecting at least 3 ft forward from the light, so as to prevent the lights being seen across the bows.

Stern light

All vessels when under way are fitted at the stern with a white light, usually at the same height as the side lights. This light is to show an unbroken light over an arc of the horizon of 12 points of the compass (135 degrees) so fixed as to show the light 67½ degrees from right aft on each side of the vessel. The light to be visible at a distance of at least two miles.

Anchor lights

All vessels 150 ft in length and above, when at anchor, must carry two white lights, capable of being visible all round the horizon at a distance of at least three miles. One light is to be forward at least 20 ft above the hull and one at or near the stern and not less than 15 ft below the forward light.

Between sunrise and sunset, when at anchor, every vessel is to carry forward, where it can best be seen, one black ball, not less than 2 ft in diameter.

Not under command lights

When a vessel is not under command two red lights are hoisted in a vertical line one over the other not less than 6 ft apart. These lights to be so constructed as to be visible all round the horizon at a distance of at least two miles. By day the lanterns are replaced by two black balls or shapes in a vertical line one over the other not less than 6 ft apart and each not less than 2 ft in diameter.

Towing lights

A vessel when towing another carries two bright white lights, in addition to the side lights, one above the other, 6 ft apart, one light being in the position of the foremost masthead light. If a second vessel is being towed, and the length of the tow is more than 600 ft from the stern of the towing vessel to the stern of the last vessel towed, a third light is carried and the lowest light of the three must not be less than 14 ft above the hull.

The statutory equipment of the lanterns used for navigation are of the oil burning type and conform to an approved design; the electric lanterns usually fitted are an addition to the statutory requirements of the regulations.

SOUND SIGNALS

Bells and gongs

All power-driven vessels must be provided with an efficient bell, hung forward clear of all obstructions and not less than 12 in diameter at the mouth, except on vessels under 150 ft in length when a bell of not less than 8 in diameter may be fitted. All vessels more than 350 ft in length must have, in addition to the bell, a gong or other instrument the tone and sounding of which cannot be confused with that of the bell. The most suitable instrument has been found to be a 16 SWG mild-steel gong not less than 16 in diameter with a lip of 2 in. Precautions against corrosion should be taken, but the gong should not be painted. The instrument should be mounted clear of all obstructions in the after part of the vessel.

Whistles and fog-horns

All power-driven vessels must have an efficient whistle, sounded by steam or some substitute for steam, and so placed that the sound cannot be intercepted by any obstruction. The whistle should be forward of the foremost funnel and above all deck-houses. A whistle is not normally regarded as efficient unless it is audible for at least two miles in a still condition of the atmosphere. Ordinary 'organ' whistles should, except on vessels under 150 ft in length, be not less than 30 in high and 5 in diameter. Compressed air whistles are acceptable provided they have the range of audibility given above. Efficient electric whistles are accepted provided that:

(a) the ship has an alternative source of electrical power which may be a second generator and

(b) in the case of passenger ships it is possible for the power for the whistle to be taken from the emergency generator.

All power-driven vessels must have an efficient fog-horn sounded by mechanical means.

The signals in fog, mist, snow and heavy rainstorms or any other condition similarly restricting visibility are as follows:

A power-driven vessel making way through the water, sounds at intervals of not more than two minutes, a prolonged blast.

A vessel under way, but stopped and making no way through the water, sounds at intervals of not more than two minutes two prolonged blasts, with an interval of about one second between them.

A vessel when at anchor, gives a warning by the ringing of the bell rapidly for about five seconds, at intervals of not more than one minute. In vessels of more than 350 ft in length the bell is sounded in the fore part of the vessel, and, in addition at intervals of not more than one minute for about five seconds, a gong is sounded in the after part of the vessel. Every vessel at anchor may in addition sound three blasts in succession, namely, one short, one prolonged and one short blast to give warning of her position and of the possibility of collision to an approaching vessel.

Signalling lamp

All ships engaged on international voyages are provided with an efficient signalling lamp capable of being used both by day and by night.

Distress signals

When a vessel is in distress and requires assistance from other vessels or from the shore the following signals are used or displayed either together or separately:

(a) A gun or other explosive signal fired at intervals of about a minute.

(b) A continuous sounding with any fog-signal apparatus.

(c) Rockets or shells, throwing red stars fired one at a time at short intervals.

(d) A signal made by radiotelegraphy or other signalling method.

(e) A signal sent by radiotelephony consisting of the spoken word 'Mayday'.

(f) The International Code Signal of distress indicated by NC.

(g) A signal consisting of a square flag having above or below it a ball or anything resembling a ball.

(h) Flames on the vessel—as from a burning tar or oil barrel.

(i) A rocket parachute flare showing a red light.

A radio signal has been provided for use by vessels in distress for the purpose of actuating the auto-alarms of other vessels and thus securing attention to distress calls or messages. The signal consists of a series of 12 dashes, sent in one minute, the duration of each dash being four seconds, and the duration of the interval between two consecutive dashes one second.

Wireless

All passenger and cargo ships of 1600 tons gross and over are fitted with wireless apparatus. The advantages of wireless are many.

(a) It is possible to obtain assistance from other ships in the event of an emergency without having to depend upon visual signals.

(b) Weather reports can be received from different parts of the world.

(c) Wireless can be used as a means of checking position.

(d) Time signals can be picked up.

(e) Distress signals can be picked up from other ships.

Navigation equipment

From the navigational point of view the safety of a ship under way depends on the ability of the personnel to (1) determine accurately the position of the ship (2) keep the ship on the desired course (3) determine the presence of other ships in the vicinity and (4) make other vessels aware of her own presence. In order to accomplish these objectives the ship must be fitted with essential navigating equipment. Particular items of navigating equipment are specified by international agreement and for these the primary purpose is to ensure that equipment such as navigation lights and sound signals are uniform and recognisable by all ships. Other navigational aids are left to the discretion of the owner; owners are quick to adopt and put into practice the latest improvements in navigating equipment.

Compasses

Every ship has to be provided with magnetic compasses, the number depending upon the class of ship. One of the defects of the magnetic compass is that it records magnetic north and not true north and consequently many ships carry gyro compasses. The advantage of the gyro compass is that it records true geographical north and is independent of magnetic effects. A development of this is the gyro pilot; this apparatus is able to detect deviations from the set course and to apply automatically the correct amount of helm to set the ship on the right course.

Radio direction finder

The Convention requires that all ships of 1600 tons gross and over be fitted with a radio direction finder. It is of great value in determining a ship's position from established radio beacons.

Radar

In reduced visibility the need for radar plotting as an aid to the avoidance of collision is generally conceded. It has become an essential item of navigating equipment.

Depth-sounding apparatus

The correct determination of the depth of water in which the ship is sailing is important in preventing the ship from going aground particularly when navigating close to land. Echo sounding apparatus is now extensively used. The system consists in sending out a sound impulse directed downwards and receiving the echo from the bottom of the sea. Since sound travels at a definite speed through water the time interval between sending the impulse and receiving the echo measures twice the depth of water at that position. The equipment can give an automatic graph record of the depth of the water under the ship.

Other important aids to ships are the warnings of gales and tropical storms by radio and the daily weather bulletins. There is also the ice patrol which observes ice conditions in the North Atlantic.

Crew accommodation

The various British Merchant Shipping Acts contain certain requirements regarding the accommodation of officers and crew on board all merchant ships. Although these requirements are associated with tonnage measurement they must be complied with in all British ships. The current British regulations relating to accommodation for merchant ships are given in Statutory Instrument 1953 No. 1036—'The Merchant Shipping (crew accommodation) Regulations'. A handbook for guidance is also published by HM Stationery Office—*Crew Accommodation in Merchant Ships*. These regulations state the minimum requirements which must be complied with. It should not, however, be assumed that all shipowners have limited themselves to a standard required by law. In many modern ships a great deal of attention has been paid to crew accommodation and the welfare of the crew. This is very evident in the treatment of the living spaces for officers and crew in ships of all types built in this country in recent years.

The ship is home and club to the seafarer and in the present-day ship ample provision is made for the comfort, privacy and community life of seagoing personnel. It is quite usual to find a high proportion of a ship's complement accommodated in single-berth cabins and well-appointed recreation and smoke rooms are provided. The cabins allotted to officers, engineers and navigators are comparable with those for passengers. The single- and two-berth rooms for the crew are today, in many cases, not unlike those assigned to passengers of not so many years ago. The subject of crew accommodation in merchant ships has been deliberated at the leading technical institutions, and the proposals made have been lacking neither in vision nor imagination.

At one time the usual place for crew's quarters was in the fore-castle but under current regulations relating to accommodation suitable spaces above the load waterline, either amidships or aft of this position, must be provided. The importance of crew accommodation is apparent from the regulations which specify that a plan of the ship on a scale not less than 1 in 100 has to be submitted not later than the day on which the keel is laid. This plan has to show the proposed arrangement of the crew accommo-dation and its position relative to other spaces. Moreover, plans have to be submitted not later than the day on which construction of any part of the crew accommodation is begun showing clearly the purpose of each space and the position of furnishings, fittings and obstructions. In addition plans have to be submitted indicating the proposed arrangements for supplying water, heating, lighting and ventilation to the accommodation.

Before the arrangement of the accommodation can be developed the number of persons in the various departments has to be decided. The number on deck service depends upon the size of the ship and of those in the machinery spaces on the power and type of the propelling unit. The number on the catering staff is based on that of the crew and, of course, on the presence of passengers. The make up of the complement in a typical dry cargo ship and also for an oil tanker is given in Table 4.

The regulations relating to accommodation require the spaces to be readily accessible and able to provide protection from the weather and the sea and so arranged that adjacent spaces in which are stored offensive cargo, stores or fuel can cause no danger or discomfort to the occupants. The accommodation must have an approved system of lighting, both natural and artificial, and be

TABLE 4

	CARGO MOTORSHIP Deadweight = 9000 Tons B.H.P. = 4500	OIL TANKER STEAMSHIP Dwt = 44000 Tons S.H.P. = 16000
Captain	1	1
Navigating Officers	4	4
Wireless Operator	1	2
Engineer Officers	7	10
Electrical Engineers	2	1
Cadets	2	2
Chief Steward	1	1
Assistant Steward	6	7
Chief Cook	1	1
Assistant Cook	1	1
Boys	2	2
Bosun	1	1
Carpenter	1	1
Donkeyman	–	1
Seamen	10	17
Greasers	7	9
Storekeepers	–	2
Pumpmen	–	2
Total Complement	47	65

adequately heated and ventilated. Separate sleeping quarters must be provided for officers, petty officers, apprentices and ratings of the deck, engine room and catering departments. Each division must have messrooms, washrooms and sanitary arrangements for its exclusive use. This does not apply to apprentices if they are housed with officers and able to use their facilities.

The number of persons in sleeping rooms for officers and petty officers is one person per room; for apprentices, not more than three persons per room, for other ratings where practicable two or three persons per room and for cargo ships the maximum is four persons per room. Each watch of ratings is to be provided with sleeping rooms separate from those of other watches. In addition to the bed, which for ratings must not be less than 6 ft 3 in by 2 ft 3 in each rating is to have one drawer, a wardrobe, a table, adequate seating, a mirror, toilet cabinet, book rack, floor runner and side scuttle curtains. Messrooms must have sufficient tables to permit a space of 20 in for each person using the room. Each table at least 24 in wide if seats are on both sides and 15 in wide if seats on one side only. Single chairs to be provided for each person. Settees may replace chairs adjacent to a bulkhead or the side of the ship.

Washing facilities have to be reasonably close to the sleeping rooms, the washrooms to contain baths with hot and cold water. The washbasins for ratings need not have hot and cold water laid on if spring loaded draw-off taps are provided. All baths, showers and basins must be fitted with an efficient and hygienic discharge system. For each of the classes of persons specified in the regulations, water closets have to be provided on the basis of one for every eight persons in each class.

An hospital must be provided with a private water closet and wash basin, and at least one single-tier bed accessible from both sides and from the foot. The minimum width of entrance has to be 30 in to permit easy entrance of a stretcher case.

Every ship of 3000 tons gross and over must have two separate rooms for use as offices and appropriately furnished for that purpose. One is for the chief officer or the officers of the deck department, and the other for the chief engineer or officers of his department. Also in ships of 3000 tons gross and over, a smoking room must be provided for the officers and it is not to be combined with a messroom. Recreation accommodation has to be provided in a messroom or elsewhere for ratings. Space has also to be arranged on an open deck for the use of the crew for recreational purposes.

Washing troughs have to be provided to enable the crew to deal with their laundry and the troughs must have an adequate supply of hot and cold fresh water. These facilities are to be a room set aside only as a laundry. Drying rooms for the crew's clothes are to be fitted with racks or rods and the heating of these rooms must be capable of being controlled independently of the heating of any other space in the ship. Adequately ventilated compartments or lockers have to be provided for hanging oilskins and working clothes used by the crew, and separate compartments or lockers arranged for officers.

The galley must be situated as near as possible to the messrooms provided for the crew and be fitted out with the necessary equipment. Storerooms for dry provisions have to be provided complete with shelves and bins. Refrigerating equipment and cold storerooms are also to be fitted.

No accommodation provided in compliance with the regulations can be used, or appropriated for use, by passengers.

Photographs of some of the accommodation spaces in a cargo ship are shown in Figures 56 to 60.

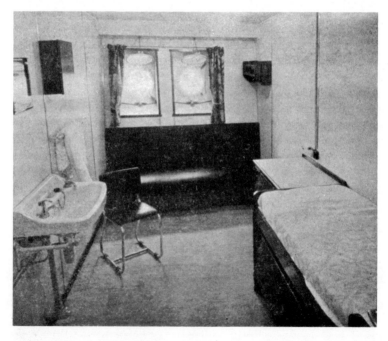

56 Single-berth crew cabin

57 Crew's messroom

58 Dining saloon

59 Smoke room

60 Captain's day room

Passenger accommodation

The Merchant Shipping Acts contain certain requirements also regarding passenger accommodation. A summary of these requirements for foreign-going passenger ships—Class I—is now given.

Passengers must not be carried on more than one deck below the waterline and berthed passengers must not normally be accommodated within one-eighth of the registered length of the ship from the fore-side of the stem. Where passenger accommodation is adjacent to cargo spaces, bunkers, lamp rooms, etc., it must be separated from such spaces by gastight steel bulkheads and decks.

All passenger accommodation must be efficiently ventilated and lighted during both day and night. Natural lighting should normally be provided where circumstances permit. If, however, natural lighting in any space is impracticable, such space may be accepted if suitably lighted by artificial means. Passenger accommodation must be fitted with efficient heating arrangements.

The number of properly constructed fixed berths fitted for passengers determines the number of passengers to be allowed in each class if a reasonable amount of floor space in the sleeping rooms for each passenger is provided. There should not be more than two tiers of berths in any cabin. The total space excluding airing space allocated for the exclusive use of passengers must be such as to provide at least 36 clear superficial feet per passenger. In assessing the total space all enclosed spaces such as saloons and recreation rooms, etc., allocated to each class are included.

Accommodation layout

As there is just so much space on a given ship which can be made available to passengers it is important to proportion to it to the best advantage between cabins, public rooms and outside spaces. The amount of space provided per passenger depends to a great extent upon the service of the ship. For example in the cross-channel type, where the journey is short, much less space is necessary than in the ship on a voyage of days or weeks. Probably the highest standard of accommodation is reached in the Atlantic liner.

Access is the key to passenger ship accommodation layout. Access is the ability of the crew and passengers to get about the ship in a simple and direct manner. If the ship is multi-class consideration should be given to the possibility of the vessel 'cruising'. Such ships are frequently used as one class and as a result the access aspect becomes important.

In general the accommodation may be arranged round a main entrance which gives access by way of stairways and lifts to the various decks on which the cabins and public rooms are situated.

Cabins

The objective in the layout is to care for the comfort and well-being of the passengers. The arrangement should include all the requirements of a cabin in the smallest space in keeping with comfort, ease of movement and elegant appearance. Part of a two-berth passengers' suite is shown in Figure 61.

61 Part of a de-luxe suite

Public rooms

The requirements here are to provide centres for social activities and entertainment in addition to dining saloons. The facilities include lounges, smoke rooms, writing rooms, bars, theatre, etc. As public rooms are noisy they should be kept apart from the state rooms. It is fairly common to locate most public rooms on one deck, the promenade deck and not to have cabins at that level. There is often to be found a gymnasium and a swimming pool. Shopping facilities are available in many ships and these are usually located in the main entrance.

Promenade spaces

These are generally in the form of a loop with a screen at the forward end to protect walkers against the breeze. Windows are fitted at the forward end and sides of the screen. As the promenade space has normally deck chairs it is desirable that this space be as wide as possible. Open deck areas are necessary for deck games.

Galley

An important passenger service is the preparation and service of food and great care is taken in the layout and equipment of the galley and the associated store rooms so as to ensure a high standard of service.

Officers and crew in a 'Queen' liner

The many and varied categories of personnel employed in the operation and services to passengers on board the world's largest liners are strikingly shown in Table 5 reproduced from *Cunard News*. The ship is the *Queen Elizabeth*.

Anchors and chain cables

All anchors exceeding 168 lb in weight (inclusive of stock, if fitted) and chain cables bought or sold in the United Kingdom

N

TABLE 5

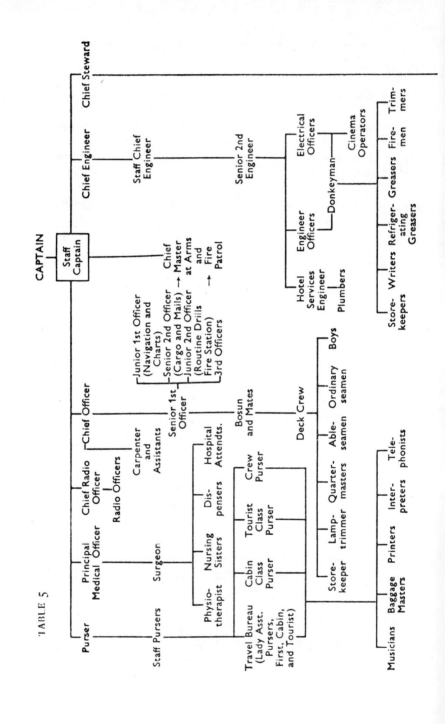

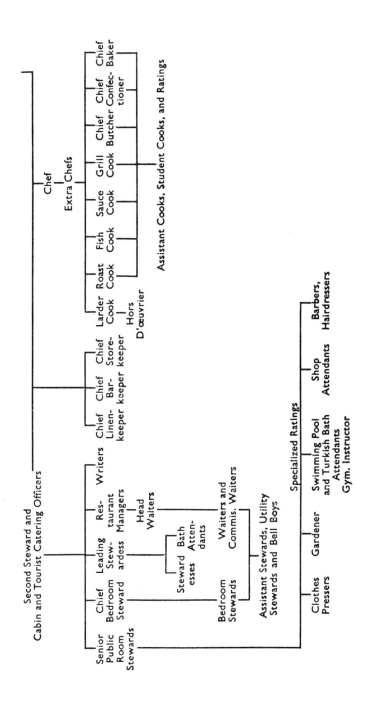

Second Steward and
Cabin and Tourist Catering Officers

Chef
Extra Chefs

Assistant Cooks, Student Cooks, and Ratings

Larder Cook — Roast Cook — Fish Cook — Sauce Cook — Grill Cook — Chief Butcher — Chief Confectioner — Chief Baker

Hors D'œuvrier

Chief Linenkeeper — Chief Barkeeper — Chief Storekeeper

Senior Public Room Stewards — Chief Bedroom Steward — Leading Stewardesses — Restaurant Managers — Writers

Head Waiters

Stewardesses — Bath Attendants

Bedroom Stewards — Waiters and Commis. Waiters

Assistant Stewards, Utility Stewards and Bell Boys

Specialized Ratings

Clothes Pressers — Gardener — Swimming Pool and Turkish Bath Attendants — Shop Attendants — Barbers, Hairdressers

Gym. Instructor

62 'Byers' patent stockless anchor

and intended to be fitted to a ship of British registry in the U.K. must be tested at a Licensed Proving House in the U.K. in accordance with the Anchors and Chain Cables Act of 1889.

The licence for establishing statutory Proving Houses is granted by the Board of Trade under the terms of the above Act and the present Public Proving Establishments in the U.K. operate under a licence granted to Lloyd's Register of Shipping and under their superintendence for testing. The Proving Houses are situated at the following towns, viz. Netherton (near Dudley), Low Walker on Tyne, Burnbank and Cardiff.

There are also a large number of establishments situated in different parts of the world which are recognised by Lloyd's Register of Shipping for the purpose of testing anchors and cables intended for ships of other than British registry.

Anchors which form part of the statutory equipment on ships classed with Lloyd's Register of Shipping are made of forged ingot steel or cast steel. Each important part of an anchor is to be plainly marked by the maker 'forged steel' or 'cast steel' as the case may be. Forged and cast steel anchor heads and cast steel shanks are to be subjected to tests specified in the Rules. All steel castings are to be subjected to hammering tests as follows: All castings are to be slung up and well hammered to satisfy the surveyors that the casting is sound and without flaw. For large castings the hammer used for this test is to be not less than 7 lb weight. The test load for anchors is tabulated in the Rules.

A 'Byers' patent stockless anchor is shown in Figure 62.

Chain cable

All chain cable on ships classed with Lloyd's has to be tested at a proving establishment approved by the Society. When the (United Kingdom) Anchors and Chain Cables Act applies the cables are to be tested at a licensed proving house in the United Kingdom.

Among the tests are: (a) Proof loading test. Each length of chain cable is subjected to a proof loading test in an approved testing machine and is to withstand a specified load appropriate to the grade and size of cable. (b) Breaking test. Specimens have to withstand a specified load appropriate to the grade and size of cable. Specimens are considered to have passed the test if they show no sign of fracture after application of the load.

When the (United Kingdom) Anchors and Chain Cables Act applies one three-link sample is taken from every 15 fathoms or less length and subjected to a specified breaking load.

Equipment

The Board of Trade do not specify the number or size of anchors, or the length of chain cable to be carried on ships.

All ships classed with a Classification Society must be supplied with a sufficient quantity of chain cable, an approved number of anchors, and a sufficient length of tow line and mooring lines, if the owner desires to have the appropriate equipment symbol added to the classification symbol or character of the ship.

The figure 1 in the character assigned to a vessel classed with Lloyd's Register of Shipping, thus ✠ 100 A1 indicates that the equipment of anchors, chain cables and hawsers is in accordance with Rule requirements. When the equipment of a ship is not supplied or maintained in accordance with the requirements of the Rules but is considered by the Society to be acceptable for the particular service, the figure 1 may be omitted and a line inserted after the character, thus ✠ 100A–. In cases where the equipment is found to be seriously deficient in quality or quantity, the class of the ship is liable to be withheld from the Register Book.

The equipment of anchors, cables and lines depends upon an 'Equipment Number' which is calculated as follows:

$$\text{Equipment Number} = 1 \cdot 012 \, \triangle^{\frac{2}{3}} + \frac{B \times h}{5 \cdot 382} + \frac{A}{107 \cdot 64}$$

where

$\triangle$ =moulded displacement, in tons to the summer load waterline.

B =greatest moulded breadth, in feet

h =effective height, in feet, from the summer load waterline to the top (at side) of the uppermost house having a breadth greater than B/4

A =area, in square feet, in profile view, of the hull, superstructures and houses above the summer load waterline, which are within the rule length of the vessel, and also having a width greater than B/4.

In the calculation of h, sheer and trim are ignored, i.e. h is the sum of the freeboard amidships plus the height (at side) of each tier of houses having a breadth greater than B/4.

If a house having a breadth greater than B/4 is above a house with a breadth of B/4 or less, then the wide house is to be included, but the narrow house ignored.

Screens and bulwarks more than 4 ft 11 in in height are regarded as parts of houses when determining h and A.

Associated with, and corresponding to, the equipment number in the Rules is an 'Equipment Letter' which is recorded in the Register Book together with the other particulars of the ship.

Chain cable may be of wrought iron, mild steel, special quality steel, special quality cast steel or extra special quality steel in accordance with the Society requirements.

A 'stud' is inserted by being pressed into position between the link, which gives support and prevents the sides of the link from collapsing. This is what is termed 'stud-link chain cable'.

When chain cable is worn and the mean diameter at the part most worn has been reduced to a minimum size given in the Rules, it must be renewed.

Tow lines and mooring lines may be of wire, natural fibre or synthetic fibre material, or of a mixture of wire and either natural or synthetic fibre.

IX · REGULATIONS FOR SAFETY OF LIFE AT SEA

The standard of safety applicable to passenger ships has been determined by various International Conferences. The Convention resulting from the 1948 Conference on Safety of Life at Sea has been made law by almost all maritime countries. A further International Conference in 1960 on safety of Life at Sea embodies the latest recommendations and requirements in a new Convention.

There are three lines of defence adopted in the construction and equipment of a ship which constitute the main means of protection from the hazards of the sea. Under peacetime conditions the main risks associated with merchant ships are those of collision and grounding. The first line of defence is to so design the ship with a system of watertight compartments that should the hull be pierced by collision or disabled by some other form of casualty there will be a good chance that the ship will remain afloat for some time. The benefits of subdividing ships by transverse bulkheads has always been recognised. The functions of bulkheads and the classification rules for cargo ships are dealt with in Chapter II.

Watertight subdivision of passenger ships

For a passenger ship the internal subdivision is laid down by international convention. Passenger ships are defined in the

Merchant Shipping Acts as those carrying more than 12 passengers. In the Merchant Shipping Act of 1854 the first reference is made to the recognition of a system of bulkhead subdivision in British merchant ships. The requirements in the Act were eventually looked upon as unsatisfactory and were repealed in 1862. The disastrous loss of the *Titanic* on her maiden voyage in 1912, as the result of a collision with an iceberg, when 1490 people lost their lives, was the cause of directing public attention to the subject of safety of life at sea, and prompted the British Government to appoint a committee to advise on the watertight subdivision of passenger ships. An extensive investigation was carried out under the supervision of Professor Welch of Armstrong College, now the University of Newcastle upon Tyne, and the findings have formed the basis of all statutory subdivision calculations for passenger ships ever since.

The effects of damage which destroys the watertightness of a ship's hull are often progressive. They depend upon the extent of damage in relation to the ship's internal arrangement and the type and extent of any cargo in the damaged compartments. The extent of flooding in any compartment depends upon the amount of empty space in the compartment.

If a ship consisted of a single compartment then if the hull is pierced the vessel would, in time, be flooded from end to end and the ship would sink. If, however, the ship is subdivided by transverse watertight bulkheads, then, when damage occurs, flooding is restricted to the compartment in which the damage takes place. The ship, of course, loses buoyancy due to damage and will sink deeper in the water but collecting buoyancy from the above water portion of the hull. The provision of a certain minimum freeboard ensures that there is some reserve buoyancy. The ship not only sinks in the water but also trims by the bow or the stern depending upon whether the damaged compartment is forward or aft. After damage, the water level rises inside the ship until the levels inside and outside are identical. Should this level be above the tops of the bulkheads, that is above the deck at which the bulkheads terminate, then water is no longer restricted to the compartment in which damage has taken place since the pressure of water can force off hatches, and the water has then free access to 'tween

deck spaces and other hold spaces so that the ship would eventually sink. It is thus evident as a first principle that the subdivision arrangements in a ship should be such as to prevent the
'bulkhead deck' being submerged when a compartment is damaged
and open to the sea.

The broad principles underlying the regulations for the subdivision of passenger ships can be stated as follows:

(1) A passenger ship is one which carries more than 12 passengers.
Ships carrying 12 passengers or less do not come within the
provisions of the Convention.

(2) The degree of subdivision into watertight compartments
varies according to the nature of the service of the ship and its
length on the load waterline.

(3) The highest standard of subdivision is applied to a ship
primarily engaged in the carrying of passengers and is gradually
reduced in order to suit a ship which comes close to the purely
cargo type.

When the requirements have been complied with a mark is
placed permanently on the ship's sides amidships, representing
the permissible draught to which the ship can be loaded, this is
known as the approved 'subdivision loadline'. The letter C is
placed at the passenger load line. By the regulations ships having
spaces which are adapted for the accommodation of passengers
and the carriage of cargo alternatively may have, if the owners
desire, one or more additional load lines assigned and marked
corresponding to the subdivision draughts approved for the
alternative condition. The notation C_1 is used for the deepest subdivision load-line, and the notations C_2, C_3, etc., for the alternative
conditions of service. An illustration of the variation in the markings is shown in Figure 63. In no case may any subdivision load
line be assigned and marked on the ship's sides above the deepest
load-line in sea water determined by the load-line Rules.

The 'bulkhead deck' is the uppermost deck to which the transverse watertight bulkheads are carried and forms the upper
boundary of the intact superstructure. The 'margin line' is a line
drawn parallel to and 3 in below the upper surface of the bulkhead
deck at side and is the line beyond which the ship should not sink
when the hull is pierced. The bulkhead deck and the margin line

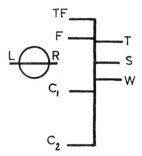

63 Freeboard markings

are shown in Figure 64. The method adopted is to ascertain the position and length of the compartment which when flooded will cause sinkage to the margin line.

The volumes contained between the proposed watertight bulkheads are calculated to the moulded lines—that is, the designed lines showing the form of the ship—from the side and bottom shell plating up to the margin line. The effect of these volumes on the

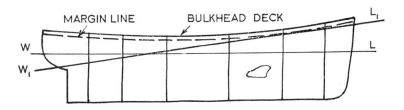

64 Bulkhead deck and margin line

calculation depends upon the permeability of the compartment. The percentage volume of a space that can be flooded is known as the permeability. In any flooded space the volume of water which can be admitted will depend upon whether the space is empty, or, if it is filled with cargo, then upon the nature of the cargo. If a compartment is filled with sponges then such a cargo would have a very high permeability, perhaps 90 per cent. If a compartment is filled with baulks of timber of square cross-section and closely packed, then such a cargo would have a very low permeability, perhaps 20 per cent. In the calculations the permeability of passenger spaces and crew spaces are taken as 95, that for cargo and store spaces as 60 and that for double bottom and oil fuel tanks as 95. The average permeability of the machinery space and the uniform average permeability of the spaces forward and aft of the machinery space are obtained by the application of an approved formula.

There are a number of important features about the form of the ship which are essential for the calculation. Such as the shape of the under-water portion; the ratio of the freeboard to the draught desired; the form of the mean waterplane between the load waterplane and that drawn parallel thereto and touching the margin line; the amount of sheer of the bulkhead deck. These items have a very direct bearing on the calculations under consideration.

The Bulkhead Committee prepared, as a basis for comparison with ships of varying length and form, a series of curves based on a ship of standard form, one set of curves calculated on a permeability of 100 and the other based on a permeability of 60. Knowing the values of the features listed above—sheer, freeboard ratio, etc.—it is possible from these curves to plot a curve of 'floodable lengths' for a particular ship. Such a curve is shown in Figure 65.

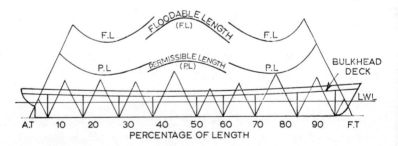

65 Floodable and permissible lengths

The 'floodable length' is the maximum length of a compartment which can be flooded so as to bring a damaged ship to float at a waterline tangential to the margin line. A curve of floodable length is one which at every point in its length has an ordinate representing the length of the ship which may be flooded with the centre of the length at that point, without the margin line being submerged. If the flooded compartment is amidships the ship will sink to a waterline parallel to the original waterline. If, however, the damaged compartment is at the ends of the ship the new waterline will be at an inclination to the original waterline as is indicated in Figure 64. The tendency to bring this waterline as a tangent to the margin line is much greater than if the same length of compartment were at amidships. This, in fact, means that the lengths of the compartments are reduced towards the ends of the ship.

The ordinates of the flooding curves are modified for any difference of form between the actual and the standard ship, and still further modified by the use of an appropriate 'factor of subdivision'. This factor depends on the length of the ship, and for a given length varies according to the nature of the service for which the ship is intended. It decreases in a regular and continuous manner as:

(a) the length increases
(b) the number of passengers increases
(c) the number of passengers below the margin line increases.

This means that as the factor decreases the standard of subdivision increases. A factor of subdivision of unity means that the transverse watertight bulkheads are so situated that if any one of the compartments is open to the sea, all assumed conditions being satisfied, the ship will not be immersed beyond the margin line. Similarly a ship having a factor of subdivision of 0·5 is one in which any two adjoining compartments may be open to the sea and the vessel remains afloat. If the factor is 0·33 then the vessel will float with three adjacent compartments open to the sea.

The result of the foregoing modifications is to produce another curve called the 'curve of permissible' lengths. This is shown in Figure 65. The length of any one compartment must not extend above the curve of permissible lengths.

The flooding calculation is carried out on the basis of a draught or freeboard specified by the owner for the intended service of the ship.

Stability in damaged condition

The Convention requires a passenger ship to have sufficient stability in all service conditions, thus enabling it to withstand the final stage of flooding of any one watertight compartment, which is required to be within the floodable length. Where the required factor of subdivision is 0·50 or less the intact stability shall be adequate to withstand the flooding of any two adjacent main compartments. The initial stability of the ship is deemed to be sufficient if, after the assumed damage and after equalising flooding measures have been taken, the final condition of the ship is as follows:

(a) In the event of symmetrical flooding the metacentric height is positive.

(b) In the event of unsymmetrical flooding the angle of heel does not exceed seven degrees.

(c) In the event of unsymmetrical flooding the margin line is not submerged.

Every passenger ship must be inclined upon its completion and the elements of stability determined. The ship's master must be supplied with stability data for the ship and this must include information regarding stability in the damaged condition. The nature, amount and distribution of any permanent ballast is to be recorded in the appropriate form. Details of the inclining experiment and other aspects of STABILITY are given in Chapter V.

Protection of ship against fire

The Convention requires provision to be made in passenger ships to prevent or retard the spread of fire. The means adopted may be divided into three parts namely (a) fire-proofing the ship as far as possible, (b) means for detecting a fire where and when it occurs and (c) means for extinguishing fires.

Below the bulkhead deck the transverse watertight bulkheads, due to their spacing, will confine a fire within comparatively small limits. In passenger ships the risk of fire spreading throughout the ship is reduced by dividing the ship into vertical zones by means of fire-resisting bulkheads which extend from side to side of the ship and are not more than 131 ft apart. These fire-resisting bulk-heads are required to be of steel or similar material and capable of preventing the passage of smoke and flame throughout a standard fire test of one hour. These are called 'A' class divisions. As openings may be required in these fire-resisting bulkheads, fireproof doors must be fitted which are themselves able to resist the passage of smoke or flame and which can be closed readily in an emergency and opened by one person on either side of the bulkhead. There is also a class 'B' division which must be capable of preventing the passage of smoke and flame throughout a standard fire test of 30 minutes' duration.

The accommodation spaces and service spaces have to be con-structed in accordance with one of the following methods of fire protection:

Method 1. Internal bulkheads of 'B' class divisions together with an automatic fire alarm and fire detection system in these spaces.

Method II. The fitting of an automatic sprinkler, fire-detection and fire-alarm system in the accommodation and service spaces.

Method III. The subdivision of the spaces by 'A' class and 'B' class divisions, together with the fitting of an automatic fire alarm and fire-detection system in all the spaces and a restriction of combustible material in these spaces.

In order to detect a fire which may occur on board a pas-senger ship a patrol system is maintained through all accessible spaces and manual fire alarms are provided so that the fire patrol can give the alarm to the bridge or to the fire-control station. The fire-alarm or fire-detection system enables the presence of a fire in the inaccessible places of the vessel to be observed in one or more positions in the ship. In addition to portable fire extinguishers the fire-fighting appliances include means for directing jets of water on to any part of the deck or space used by passengers or crew when all watertight doors and doors in fire-resisting bulkheads are closed. In addition provision is made for directing water jets into any cargo space and the machinery spaces. In ships above a certain size the Convention requires arrangements so that fire-smothering gas can be rapidly conveyed by a permanent piping system into the cargo spaces.

Special arrangements are required in the machinery spaces.

LIFE-SAVING APPLIANCES

Lifeboats

As it is not possible to legislate for all the perils of the sea it is thus necessary to provide ships with life-saving appliances so that passengers and crew can leave the ship in safety in the event of the ship sinking or of there being a dangerous fire on board. This is the second line of defence against the casualty at sea and consists of lifeboats with davits, which can be launched overboard quickly and lowered safely into the water within a reasonable time.

The main difference between a passenger and a cargo ship in regard to safety equipment lies in the provision made for lifeboats. In a cargo ship all the persons on board can be accommodated in boats under davits on 'each side' of the ship. In a passenger ship the full accommodation for all persons on board is provided in boats stowed under davits on 'both sides' of the ship. These requirements may, at first sight, appear to give a higher standard of safety to the cargo ship, but it should be borne in mind that the passenger ship must comply with high subdivision requirements and in general is much more able to keep afloat after damage than the cargo ship. Moreover, it would be difficult, if not impossible, to provide in the passenger ship boats for everyone on board on each side of the ship, and at the same time arrange them so that they could be handled quickly and efficiently.

In passenger ships engaged on short international voyages, the number of sets of davits to be fitted depends on the length of the ship and each set of davits must have attached to it a lifeboat. If the number of lifeboats thus provided does not give sufficient capacity for all the people on board then additional lifeboats or liferafts are to be fitted to make up the difference in capacity. These additional lifeboats must be stowed under davits. In every passenger ship there must be on each side of the ship at least one motor lifeboat. Passenger ships must also have two emergency boats, one on each side of the ship under davits and ready for immediate use whilst the ship is at sea. These emergency boats may be counted as part of the life-saving equipment in determining the number of boats required. As well as providing lifeboat accommodation it is also necessary to provide in ships on international voyages liferafts to accommodate 25 per cent of the total number of persons which the ship is certified to carry and buoyant apparatus for 3 per cent of that number.

Each ship must have one lifejacket for each person the ship is certified to carry, and also carry a number of lifebuoys determined in accordance with the length of the ship. Each ship must also have a line-throwing appliance.

Lifeboats may be constructed of wood, steel, aluminium or glass reinforced plastic, although modern lifeboats are generally made of fibreglass. All lifeboats must be of such form and proportions that they have ample stability in a seaway and sufficient freeboard when loaded with their full complement of persons and equipment.

All lifeboats must be not less than 24 ft in length except where owing to the size of the ship, or for other reasons, the Administration considers the carriage of such lifeboats unreasonable or impracticable. In no ship shall the lifeboats be less than 16 ft in

TABLE 6 FIBREGLASS LIFEBOATS

DIMENSIONS	PERSONS	DAVIT LOAD Cwts.	NOTES
16′ ×6′ ×2′ 4¾	14	33	The fitting of an engine to
17′ ×6′ 6 ×2′ 10″	17	37	any of these boats reduces
18′ ×6′ 6″ ×2′ 10″	18	41	the number of persons by
19′ ×6′ 6″ ×2′ 11″	19	45	two but the davit load remains the same.
24′ ×8′ ×3′ 4″	42	90	mains the same.
24′ ×8′ 9″ ×3′ 11″	56	113	Davit load includes
26′ ×8′ 10″ ×3′ 11″	60	130	persons, equipment, provisions and water.
26′ ×9′ 2″ ×4′ 1½″	64	140	These boats have hand
28′ ×9′ 10″ ×4′ 4″	84	185	propelling gear. The
30′ ×10′ 6″ ×4′ 7″	92	194	fitting of an engine to
31′ ×10′ 7″ ×4′ 6″	99	208	any of these boats reduces
36′ ×12′ ×5′	146	302	the number of persons by
37′ 6″ ×12′ 6″ ×5′ 3″	150	320	five and the davit load by 3 cwt.

o

length. No lifeboat may be approved the weight of which when fully loaded exceeds 20 tons or has a carrying capacity of more than 150 persons. All lifeboats permitted to carry more than 60 persons, but not more than 100 persons shall be in either motor boats or lifeboats with means of mechanical propulsion. Lifeboats carrying more than 100 persons must be motor lifeboats.

The dimensions of fibreglass lifeboats as built by Hugh McLean & Sons Ltd of Renfrew are given in Table 6.

Lifeboats are provided with internal buoyancy tanks. All lifeboats carry a considerable amount of equipment including oars and sails, a sea anchor, a compass and various signalling devices: a supply of food and drinking water is also provided.

Davits

Extensive improvements have taken place in the design of davits for turning out and lowering the lifeboats on board ship. At one time the radial bar type was the only one available, the boats being turned out and lowered manually. A development of this type included mechanical gearing. Quite a number of patent davits have been produced in the last three decades and in general they can be divided into two classes:

(a) *Luffing davits* Those which are turned out by mechanical means.

(b) *Gravity davits* Those which are turned out and launch the boats under the action of gravity.

A Welin Crescent luffing davit is shown in Figure 66 and a Welin overhead gravity davit is shown in Figure 67. In the davits of the gravity type when the davit release has been removed the boat is swung outboard and lowered by the action of gravity. The rate of lowering is controlled by means of boat winches to which the boat falls are attached.

Reports of disasters at sea indicate that the main problem of survival is one of launching the lifeboats and other floating equipment and getting them clear of the ship's side. Lifeboats are constructed with a high degree of buoyancy, provisioned to maintain life over a reasonable period, made fire-resistant to allow them to be launched from a fire-swept deck, but this is of little avail if

66 Welin crescent luffing davit

the boats cannot be successfully launched. The launching apparatus is of prime importance and its design and construction has made considerable progress since the beginning of the century.

The simple type of round bar davits, which operated with a radial action, were at one time in universal use for boats of all sizes. In operation these davits required the boat to be pulled clear of the deck chocks and manhandled to an outboard position to be lowered by hand tackle to the water. This was by no means a simple operation, particularly under adverse weather conditions.

The first mechanically assisted boat davit was designed by the late Axel Welin and the basic design is still used today in luffing davits. The Welin davit was positioned at the ends of the stowed lifeboat, and the outboard travel was governed by a hand-cranked screw. The lower part of the arms was made to form a quadrant, toothed to engage and roll on a fixed rack in the mounting frame.

67 Welin overhead gravity davit

This type of quadrant davit was very easy to operate compared to the manhandling required with the radial type of davit. The introduction of specialised boat winches reduced still further the manual effort necessary to lower and recover lifeboats.

The davits used for lifeboat duty on sea-going ships are in two categories, as indicated above, trackway and pivoting and both have a common purpose to provide the maximum launching stability under adverse conditions.

The trackway davit, as invariably fitted to passenger vessels, permits the lifeboats to be carried clear of the deck and provides unobstructed deck space for the use of passengers. The lifeboats are carried in cradles which move on rollers within the channel flange of the tracks. As the tracks are inclined at an angle of 30 degrees the cradles will carry the boat to outboard under extreme adverse conditions of heel and trim when the boat winch brake is lifted. Trackway davits were introduced in 1927.

An unusual lifeboat stowage was adopted in the *Oriana* and *Canberra* P & O liners where the lifeboats are positioned between decks, three decks down, and a unique design of retractable trackway davits, with the lifeboats suspended on special cradles,

68 Underdeck gravity davit as on *Canberra*

enabled the boats to be stowed under all conditions of service, without any form of keel support. This arrangement is shown in Figure 68.

Pivoting davits are normally deck mounted, and in this form are not generally adopted on passenger ships where deck promenade space is of great importance.

The function of a winch serving davits, under statutory rules, is to lower the lifeboat to the water in a controlled and predictable manner. As boats are recovered from the water to the stowed position during exercises and tests, boat winches do this extra duty with a reasonable number of working crew on board. When the boat is being lowered the only manual function required is for one operator to release the hand brake and hold it at the 'off' position during the lowering period. The lowering speed is within the range of 60 to 120 ft per minute.

Inflatable liferafts are now an item of survival equipment provided that approved means of launching them is available and that the stations will be available at all times for such launching as

69 Welin liferaft davit

occasion demands. The liferaft davits available enable the rafts to be launched in a loaded condition, quickly and consecutively, even from vessels with high freeboard. The Welin Liferaft Davit is shown in Figure 69 and the liferaft test on that davit is shown in Figure 70.

70 Liferaft davit under test

Buoyant apparatus: inflatable liferafts

These constitute the third and last line of defence against casualty. They can be thrown overboard in case of necessity, to enable persons in the water to keep afloat until assistance is rendered by lifeboats.

The buoyant apparatus has to be of such construction that it retains its shape and properties when exposed to the weather on board ship and when in the water. The apparatus has to be such that it can be thrown from the place where it is stowed into the water without being damaged.

The inflatable liferaft has to be so constructed that if dropped into water from a height of 60 ft neither the liferaft nor its equipment will be damaged. The liferaft has to be fitted with a cover capable of protecting the occupants against injury from exposure and means for collecting rain have to be provided. The liferaft has to be inflated by a gas and the inflation must take place automatically either on the pulling of a line or by some other equally simple and efficient method.

Guard rails and bulwarks

Guard rails and bulwarks are provided on every deck to which any persons may have access. In ships of Class I where guard rails are fitted the top of the uppermost rail should not be less than 3 ft 6 in high and the rails not more than 9 in apart unless strong netting is provided. Where bulwarks are fitted they should be at least 3 ft 6 in high and the freeing ports therein covered by a grid or bars to prevent any person from falling through the port.

APPENDIX I · INTERNATIONAL LOAD LINE
CONVENTION (1966)

Definitions

(1) *Length.* The length (L) shall be taken as 96 per cent of the total length on a waterline at 85 per cent of the least moulded depth measured from the top of the keel, or as the length from the foreside of the stem to the axis of the rudder stock on that waterline, if that be greater.

(2) *Perpendiculars.* The forward and after perpendiculars shall be taken at the forward and after ends of the length (L). The forward perpendicular shall coincide with the foreside of the stem on the waterline on which the length is measured.

(3) *Amidships.* Amidships is at the middle of the length (L).

(4) *Breadth.* The breadth (B) is the maximum breadth of the ship, measured amidships to the moulded line of the frame.

(5) *Moulded depth.*

(a) The moulded depth is the vertical distance measured from the top of the keel to the top of the freeboard deck beam at side.

(b) In ships having rounded gunwales the moulded depth shall be measured to the point of intersection of the moulded lines of the deck and side shell plating, the lines extending as though the gunwale were of angular design.

(6) *Depth for freeboard (D)*

(a) The depth for freeboard (D) is the moulded depth amidships, plus the thickness of the freeboard deck stringer plate, where fitted, plus $\dfrac{T\,(L\text{-}S)}{L}$ if the exposed freeboard deck is sheathed, where

> T is the mean thickness of the exposed sheathing clear of deck openings, and
>
> S is the total length of superstructures as defined in sub-paragraph (10) (d) of this Regulation.

(b) The depth for freeboard (D) in a ship having a rounded gunwale with a radius greater than 4 per cent of the breadth (B) or having topsides of unusual form is the depth for freeboard of a ship having a midship section with vertical topsides and with the same round of beam and area of topside section equal to that provided by the actual midship section.

(7) *Block coefficient.* The block coefficient (C_b) is given by

$$C_b = \frac{V}{L.\,B.\,d_1} \; ; \text{ where}$$

> V is the volume of the moulded displacement of the ship, excluding bossing, at a moulded draught of d_1 and where d_1 is 85 per cent of the least moulded depth.

(8) *Freeboard.* The freeboard assigned is the distance measured vertically downwards amidships from the upper edge of the deck line to the upper edge of the related load line.

(9) *Freeboard deck.* The freeboard deck is normally the uppermost complete deck exposed to weather and sea, which has permanent means of closing all openings in the weather part thereof, and below which all openings in the sides of the ship are fitted with permanent means of watertight closing.

(10) *Superstructure*

(a) A superstructure is a decked structure on the freeboard deck, extending from side to side of the ship or with the side plating not being inboard of the shell plating more than 4 per cent of the breadth (B). A raised quarter-deck is regarded as a superstructure.

(b) An enclosed superstructure is a superstructure with

> (i) enclosing bulkheads of efficient construction.
>
> (ii) access openings, if any, in these bulkheads fitted with doors complying with the requirements of Regulation 12.

(iii) all other openings in sides or ends of the superstructure fitted with efficient weathertight means of closing.

A bridge or poop shall not be regarded as enclosed unless access is provided for the crew to reach machinery and other working spaces inside these superstructures by alternative means which are available at all times when bulkhead openings are closed.

(c) The height of a superstructure is the least vertical height measured at side from the top of the superstructure deck beams to the top of the freeboard deck beams.

(d) The length of a superstructure (S) is the mean length of the part of the superstructure which lies within the length (L).

(11) *Flush-deck ship.* A flush-deck ship is one which has no super-structure on the freeboard deck.

(12) *Weathertight.* Weathertight means that in any sea conditions water will not penetrate into the ship.

REGULATION 11

SUPERSTRUCTURE AND BULKHEADS

Bulkheads at exposed ends of enclosed superstructures shall be of efficient construction and shall be to the satisfaction of the Administration.

REGULATION 12

DOORS

(1) All access openings in bulkheads at ends of enclosed superstructures shall be fitted with doors of steel or other equivalent material, permanently and strongly attached to the bulkhead, and framed, stiffened and fitted so that the whole structure is of equivalent strength to the unpierced bulkhead and weathertight when closed. The means for securing these doors weathertight shall consist of gaskets and clamping devices or other equivalent means and shall be permanently attached to the bulkhead or to the doors themselves, and the doors shall be so arranged that they can be operated from both sides of the bulkhead.

(2) Except as otherwise provided in these Regulations, the height of the sills of access openings in bulkheads at ends of enclosed superstructures shall be at least 15 in above the deck.

REGULATION 13

POSITION OF HATCHWAYS, DOORWAYS AND VENTILATORS

For the purpose of the Regulations, two positions of hatchways, doorways and ventilators are defined as follows:

Position 1.—Upon exposed freeboard and raised quarter-decks, and upon exposed superstructure decks situated forward of a point located a quarter of the ship's length from the forward perpendicular.

Position 2.—Upon exposed superstructure decks situated abaft a quarter of the ship's length from the forward perpendicular.

REGULATION 14

CARGO AND OTHER HATCHWAYS

(1) The construction and the means for securing the weathertightness of cargo and other hatchways in positions 1 and 2 shall be at least equivalent to the requirements of Regulations 15 and 16.

(2) Coamings and hatchway covers to exposed hatchways on decks above the superstructure deck shall comply with the requirements of the Administration.

REGULATION 15

HATCHWAYS CLOSED BY PORTABLE COVERS AND SECURED WEATHERTIGHT BY TARPAULINS AND BATTENING DEVICES

Hatchway coamings

(1) The coamings of hatchways closed by portable covers secured weathertight by tarpaulins and battening devices shall be of substantial construction, and their height above the deck shall be at least as follows:

$23\frac{1}{2}$ in if in position 1.
$17\frac{1}{2}$ in if in position 2.

REGULATION 16

HATCHWAYS CLOSED BY WEATHERTIGHT COVERS OF STEEL OR OTHER EQUIVALENT MATERIAL FITTED WITH GASKETS AND CLAMPING DEVICES

Hatchway coamings

(1) At positions 1 and 2 the height above the deck of hatchway coamings fitted with weathertight hatch covers of steel or other equivalent material fitted with gaskets and clamping devices shall be as specified in Regulation 15 (1).

REGULATION 25

PROTECTION OF THE CREW

(1) The strength of the deckhouses used for the accommodation of the crew shall be to the satisfaction of the Administration.

(2) Efficient guard rails or bulwarks shall be fitted on all exposed parts of the freeboard and superstructure decks. The height of the bulwarks or guard rails shall be at least $39\frac{1}{2}$ in from the deck, provided that where this height would interfere with the normal operation of the ship, a lesser height may be approved if the Administration is satisfied that adequate protection is provided.

(3) The opening below the lowest course of the guard rails shall not exceed 9 in. The other courses shall be not more than 15 in apart. In the case of ships with rounded gunwales the guard rail supports shall be placed on the flat of the deck.

(4) Satisfactory means (in the form of guard rails, life lines, gangways or underdeck passages, etc.) shall be provided for the protection of the crew in getting to and from their quarters, the machinery space and all other parts used in the necessary work of the ship.

(5) Deck cargo carried on any ship shall be so stowed that any opening which is in way of the cargo and which gives access to and from the crew's quarters, the machinery space and all other parts used in the necessary work of the ship, can be properly closed and secured against the admission of water. Effective protection for the crew in the form of guard rails or life lines shall be provided above the deck cargo if there is no convenient passage on or below the deck of the ship.

REGULATION 26

SPECIAL CONDITIONS OF ASSIGNMENT FOR TYPE 'A' SHIPS

Machinery Casings
(1) Machinery casings on Type 'A' ships as defined in Regulation 27 shall be protected by an enclosed poop or bridge of at least standard height, or by a deckhouse of equal height and equivalent strength.

Gangway and access
(2) An efficiently constructed fore and aft permanent gangway of sufficient strength shall be fitted on Type 'A' ships at the level of the

superstructure deck between the poop and the midship bridge or deckhouse where fitted, or equivalent means of access shall be provided to carry out the purpose of the gangway, such as passages below deck. Elsewhere, and on Type 'A' ships without a midship bridge, arrangements to the satisfaction of the Administration shall be provided to safeguard the crew in reaching all parts used in the necessary work of the ship.

(3) Safe and satisfactory access from the gangway level shall be available between separate crew accommodations and also between crew accommodations and the machinery space.

Hatchways

(4) Exposed hatchways on the freeboard and forecastle decks or on the tops of expansion trunks on Type 'A' ships shall be provided with efficient watertight covers of steel or other equivalent material.

Freeing arrangements

(5) Type 'A' ships with bulwarks shall have open rails fitted for at least half the length of the exposed parts of the weather deck or other effective freeing arrangements. The upper edge of the sheer strake shall be kept as low as practicable.

(6) Where superstructures are connected by trunks, open rails shall be fitted for the whole length of the exposed parts of the freeboard deck.

FREEBOARDS

REGULATION 27

TYPES OF SHIPS

(1) For the purposes of freeboard computation ships shall be divided into Type 'A' and Type 'B'.

Type 'A' ships

(2) A Type 'A' ship is one which is designed to carry only liquid cargoes in bulk, and in which cargo tanks have only small access openings closed by watertight gasketed covers of steel or equivalent material. Such a ship necessarily has the following inherent features:

(a) high integrity of the exposed deck: and

(b) high degree of safety against flooding, resulting from the low permeability of loaded cargo spaces and the degree of subdivision usually provided.

(3) A Type 'A' ship, if over 492 ft in length, and designed to have empty compartments when loaded to her summer-load waterline, shall be able to withstand the flooding of any one of these empty compartments at an assumed permeability of 0·95, and remain afloat in a condition of equilibrium considered to be satisfactory by the Administration. In such a ship, over 738 ft in length, the machinery space shall be treated as a floodable compartment but with a permeability of 0·85.

For the guidance of Administrations the following limits may be regarded as satisfactory

(a) the final waterline after flooding is below the lower edge of any opening through which progressive flooding may take place.

(b) The maximum angle of heel due to unsymmetrical flooding is of the order of 15 degrees.

(c) The metacentric height in the flooded condition is positive.

(4) A Type 'A' ship shall be assigned a freeboard not less than that based on Table A of Regulation 28.

Type 'B' ships

(5) All ships which do not come within the provisions regarding Type 'A' ships in paragraphs (2) and (3) of this Regulation shall be considered as Type 'B' ships.

(6) Type 'B' ships, which in position 1 have hatchways fitted with hatch covers complying with the requirements of Regulation 16 shall, except as provided in paragraphs (7) to (10) inclusive of this Regulation, be assigned freeboards based on Table B of Regulation 28.

(7) Any Type 'B' ships of over 328 ft in length may be assigned freeboards less than those required under paragraph (6) of this Regulation provided that, in relation to the amount of reduction granted, the Administration is satisfied that:

(a) the measures provided for the protection of the crew are adequate;

(b) the freeing arrangements are adequate;

(c) the covers in positions 1 and 2 comply with the provisions of Regulation 16 and have adequate strength; special care being given to their sealing and securing arrangements;

(d) the ship, when loaded to her summer-load waterline, will remain afloat in a satisfactory condition of equilibrium after flooding of any single damaged compartment at an assumed permeability of 0·95 excluding the machinery space; and

(e) in such a ship, over 738 ft. in length, the machinery space shall be treated as a floodable compartment but with a permeability of 0·85.

For the guidance of Administrations in applying sub-paragraphs (d) and (e) of this paragraph the limits given in sub-paragraphs (3) (a) (b) and (c) may be regarded as satisfactory.

The relevant calculations may be based upon the following main assumptions

—the vertical extent of damage is equal to the depth of the ship;

—the penetration of damage is not more than B/5;

—no main transverse bulkhead is damaged;

—the height of the centre of gravity above the base line is assessed allowing for homogeneous loading of cargo holds, and for 50 per cent of the designed capacity of consumable fluids and stores, etc.

(8) In calculating the freeboards for Type 'B' ships which comply with the requirements of paragraph (7) of this Regulation, the values from Table B of Regulation 28 shall not be reduced by more than 60 per cent of the difference between the 'B' and 'A' tabular values for the appropriate ship lengths.

(9) The reduction in tabular freeboard allowed under paragraph (8) of this Regulation may be increased up to the total difference between the values in Table A and those in Table B of Regulation 28 on condition that the ship complies with the requirements of Regulation 26 (1), (2), (3), (5) and (6), as if it were a type 'A' ship, and further complies with the provisions of paragraph 7(a) to (d) inclusive of this Regulation except that the reference in sub-paragraph (d) to the flooding of any single damaged compartment shall be treated as a reference to the flooding of any two adjacent fore and aft compartments, neither of which is the machinery space. Also any such ship of over 738 ft in length, when loaded to her summer-load waterline, shall remain afloat in a satisfactory condition of equilibrium after flooding of the machinery space, taken alone, at an assumed permeability of 0·85.

(10) Type 'B' ships, which in position 1 have hatchways fitted with hatch covers which comply with the requirements of Regulation 15, other than paragraph (7)—pontoon covers—shall be assigned freeboards based upon the values given in Table B of Regulation 28 increased by the values given in the following table:

Freeboard increase over Tabular Freeboard for Type 'B' ships, for ships with hatch
covers not complying with Regulations 15 (7)—pontoon covers—or 16.

LENGTH OF SHIP (ft)	FREEBOARD INCREASE (in)	LENGTH OF SHIP (ft)	FREEBOARD INCREASE (in)
350 and below	2·0	510	9·6
360	2·3	520	10·0
370	2·6	530	10·4
380	2·9	540	10·7
390	3·3	550	11·0
400	3·7	560	11·4
410	4·2	570	11·8
420	4·7	580	12·1
430	5·2	590	12·5
440	5·8	600	12·8
450	6·4	610	13·1
460	7·0	620	13·4
470	7·6	630	13·6
480	8·2	640	13·9
490	8·7	650	14·1
500	9·2	660	14·3

Freeboards at intermediate lengths of ship shall be obtained by linear interpolation.

Ships above 660 ft in length shall be dealt with by the Administrations.

P

Regulation 28—Freeboard Tables

(*1*) *The Tabular Freeboard for Type 'A' ships shall be determined from the following Table:*

TABLE A FREEBOARD TABLE FOR TYPE 'A' SHIPS

LENGTH OF SHIP (ft)	FREEBOARD (in)	LENGTH OF SHIP (ft)	FREEBOARD (in)	LENGTH OF SHIP (ft)	FREEBOARD (in)
80	8·0	460	71·1	840	120·1
90	8·9	470	73·1	850	120·7
100	9·8	480	75·1	860	121·4
110	10·8	490	77·1	870	122·1
120	11·9	500	79·0	880	122·7
130	13·0	510	80·9	890	123·4
140	14·2	520	82·7	900	124·0
150	15·5	530	84·5	910	124·6
160	16·9	540	86·3	920	125·2
170	18·3	550	88·0	930	125·7
180	19·8	560	89·6	940	126·2
190	21·3	570	91·1	950	126·7
200	22·9	580	92·6	960	127·2
210	24·5	590	94·1	970	127·7
220	26·2	600	95·5	980	128·1
230	27·8	610	96·9	990	128·6
240	29·5	620	98·3	1000	129·0
250	31·1	630	99·6	1010	129·4
260	32·8	640	100·9	1020	129·9
270	34·6	650	102·1	1030	130·3
280	36·3	660	103·3	1040	130·7
290	38·0	670	104·4	1050	131·0
300	39·7	680	105·5	1060	131·4
310	41·4	690	106·6	1070	131·7
320	43·2	700	107·7	1080	132·0
330	45·0	710	108·7	1090	132·3
340	46·9	720	109·7	1100	132·6
350	48·8	730	110·7	1110	132·9
360	50·7	740	111·7	1120	133·2
370	52·7	750	112·6	1130	133·5
380	54·7	760	113·5	1140	133·8
390	56·8	770	114·4	1150	134·0
400	58·8	780	115·3	1160	134·3
410	60·9	790	116·1	1170	134·5
420	62·9	800	117·0	1180	134·7
430	65·0	810	117·8	1190	135·0
440	67·0	820	118·6	1200	135·2
450	69·1	830	119·3		

Freeboards at intermediate lengths of ship shall be obtained by linear interpolation. Ships above 1200 ft in length shall be dealt with by the Administrations.

(2) The Tabular Freeboard for Type 'B' ships shall be determined from the following Table:

TABLE B: FREEBOARD TABLE FOR TYPE 'B' SHIPS

LENGTH OF SHIP (ft)	FREEBOARD (in)	LENGTH OF SHIP (ft)	FREEBOARD (in)	LENGTH OF SHIP (ft)	FREEBOARD (in)
80	8·0	460	83·1	840	161·2
90	8·9	470	85·6	850	162·8
100	9·8	480	88·1	860	164·3
110	10·8	490	90·6	870	165·9
120	11·9	500	93·1	880	167·4
130	13·0	510	95·6	890	168·9
140	14·2	520	98·1	900	170·4
150	15·5	530	100·6	910	171·8
160	16·9	540	103·0	920	173·3
170	18·3	550	105·4	930	174·7
180	19·8	560	107·7	940	176·1
190	21·3	570	111·0	950	177·5
200	22·9	580	112·3	960	178·9
210	24·7	590	114·6	970	180·3
220	26·6	600	116·8	980	181·7
230	28·5	610	119·0	990	183·1
240	30·4	620	121·1	1000	184·4
250	32·4	630	123·2	1010	185·8
260	34·4	640	125·3	1020	187·2
270	36·5	650	127·3	1030	188·5
280	38·7	660	129·3	1040	189·8
290	41·0	670	131·3	1050	191·0
300	43·3	680	133·3	1060	192·3
310	45·7	690	135·3	1070	193·5
320	48·2	700	137·1	1080	194·8
330	50·7	710	139·0	1090	196·1
340	53·2	720	140·9	1100	197·3
350	55·7	730	142·7	1110	198·6
360	58·2	740	144·5	1120	199·9
370	60·7	750	146·3	1130	201·2
380	63·2	760	148·1	1140	202·3
390	65·7	770	149·8	1150	203·5
400	68·2	780	151·5	1160	204·6
410	70·7	790	153·2	1170	205·8
420	73·2	800	154·8	1180	206·9
430	75·7	810	156·4	1190	208·1
440	78·2	820	158·0	1200	209·3
450	80·7	830	159·6		

Freeboards at intermediate lengths of ship shall be obtained by linear interpolation. Ships above 1200 ft in length shall be dealt with by the Administration.

REGULATION 29

CORRECTION TO THE FREEBOARD FOR SHIPS UNDER 328 FT IN LENGTH

The tabular freeboard for a type 'B' ship of between 79 ft and 328 ft in length having enclosed superstructures with an effective length of up to 35 per cent of the length of the ship shall be increased by:

$$0.09\,(328-L)\,(0.35-\frac{E}{L}\,)\text{ in}$$

where L=length of ship in feet
E=effective length of superstructure in feet as defined in Regulation 35.

REGULATION 30

CORRECTION FOR BLOCK COEFFICIENT

Where the block coefficient (C_b) exceeds 0.68, the tabular freeboard specified in Regulation 28 as modified, if applicable, by Regulations 27(8), 27(10) and 29 shall be multiplied by the factor $\dfrac{C_b+0.68}{1.36}$

REGULATION 31

CORRECTION FOR DEPTH

(1) Where D exceeds $\dfrac{L}{15}$ the freeboard shall be increased by

$\left(D-\dfrac{L}{15}\right)$ R inches, where R is $\dfrac{L}{131.2}$ at lengths less than 393.6 ft and 3 at 393 ft length and above.

(2) Where D is less than $\dfrac{L}{15}$ no reduction shall be made except in a ship with an enclosed superstructure covering at least 0.6 L amidships, with a complete trunk, or combination of detached enclosed super-structures and trunks which extend all fore and aft, where the freeboard

shall be reduced at the rate prescribed in paragraph (1) of this Regulation.

(3) Where the height of superstructure or trunk is less than the standard height, the reduction shall be in the ratio of the actual to the standard height as defined in Regulation 33.

REGULATION 32

CORRECTION FOR POSITION OF DECK LINE

Where the actual depth to the upper edge of the deck line is greater or less than D, the difference between the depths shall be added to or deducted from the freeboard.

REGULATION 33

STANDARD HEIGHT OF SUPERSTRUCTURE

The standard height of a superstructure shall be as given in the following table:

STANDARD HEIGHT (in ft)

L (ft)	RAISED QUARTER-DECK	ALL OTHER SUPERSTRUCTURES
98·5 or less	3·0	5·9
246	3·9	5·9
410 or more	5·9	7·5

The standard heights at intermediate lengths of the ship shall be obtained by linear interpolation.

REGULATION 34

LENGTH OF SUPERSTRUCTURE

(1) Except as provided in paragraph (2) of this Regulation, the length of a superstructure (S) shall be the mean length of the parts of the superstructure which lie within the length (L).

(2) Where the end bulkhead of an enclosed superstructure extends in a fair convex curve beyond its intersection with the superstructure sides,

the length of the superstructure may be increased on the basis of an equivalent plane bulkhead. This increase shall be two-thirds of the fore and aft extent of the curvature. The maximum curvature which may be taken into account in determining this increase is one-half the breadth of the superstructure at the point of intersection of the curved end of the superstructure with its side.

REGULATION 35

EFFECTIVE LENGTH OF SUPERSTRUCTURE

(1) Except as provided for in paragraph (2) of this Regulation the effective length (E) of an enclosed superstructure of standard height shall be its length.

(2) In all cases where an enclosed superstructure of standard height is set in from the sides of the ship as permitted in Regulation 3(10), the effective length shall be the length modified by the ratio of b/Bs, where

'b' is the breadth of the superstructure at the middle of its length; and

'Bs' is the breadth of the ship at the middle of the length of the superstructure.

Where a superstructure is set in for a part of its length, this modification shall be applied only to the set in part.

(3) Where the height of an enclosed superstructure is less than the standard height, the effective length shall be its length reduced in the ratio of the actual height to the standard height. Where the height exceeds the standard, no increase shall be made to the effective length of the superstructure.

(4) The effective length of a raised quarter-deck, if fitted with an intact front bulkhead, shall be its length up to a maximum of 0·6L. Where the bulkhead is not intact, the raised quarter-deck shall be treated as a poop of less than standard height.

(5) Superstructures which are not enclosed shall have no effective length.

REGULATION 36

TRUNKS

(1) A trunk or similar structure which does not extend to the sides of the ship shall be regarded as efficient on the following conditions:

(a) the trunk is at least as strong as a superstructure;

(b) the hatchways are in the trunk deck, and the hatchway coamings and covers comply with the requirements of Regulations 13 to 16 inclusive and the width of the trunk deck stringer provides a satisfactory gangway and sufficient lateral stiffness. However, small access openings with watertight covers may be permitted in the freeboard deck;

(c) A permanent working platform fore and aft fitted with guard rails is provided by the trunk deck, or by detached trunks connected to superstructures by efficient permanent gangways;

(d) ventilators are protected by the trunk, by watertight covers or by other equivalent means;

(e) open rails are fitted on the weather parts of the freeboard deck in way of the trunk for at least half their length;

(f) the machinery casings are protected by the trunk, by a superstructure of at least standard height, or by a deckhouse of the same height and of equivalent strength;

(g) the breadth of the trunk is at least 60 per cent of the breadth of the ship; and

(h) where there is no superstructure, the length of the trunk is at least 0.6 L.

(2) The full length of an efficient trunk reduced in the ratio of its mean breadth to B shall be its effective length.

(3) The standard height of a trunk is the standard height of a superstructure other than a raised quarter-deck.

(4) Where the height of a trunk is less than the standard height, its effective length shall be reduced in the ratio of the actual to the standard height. Where the height of hatchway coamings on the trunk deck is less than that required under Regulation 15(1), a reduction from the actual height of trunk shall be made which corresponds to the difference between the actual and the required height of coaming.

REGULATION 37

DEDUCTION FOR SUPERSTRUCTURES AND TRUNKS

(1) Where the effective length of superstructures and trunks is 1·0 L the deduction from the freeboard shall be 14 in at 79 ft length of ship, 34 in at 279 ft length, and 42 in at 400 ft length and above; deductions at intermediate lengths shall be obtained by linear interpolation.

(2) Where the total effective length of superstructures and trunks is less than than 1 0 L the deduction shall be a percentage obtained from one of the following Tables:

PERCENTAGE OF DEDUCTION FOR TYPE 'A' SHIPS

	Total Effective length of Superstructure and Trunks										
	0	0·1 L	0·2 L	0·3 L	0·4 L	0·5 L	0·6 L	0·7 L	0·8 L	0·9 L	1·0 L
Percentage of deduction for all types of super-structures	0	7	14	21	31	41	52	63	75·5	87·7	100

PERCENTAGE OF DEDUCTION FOR TYPE 'B' SHIPS

		Total effective length of Superstructures and Trunks										
	Line	0	0·1 L	0·2 L	0·3 L	0·4 L	0·5 L	0·6 L	0·7 L	0·8 L	0·9 L	1·0 L
Ships with forecastle and without detached bridge	I	0	5	10	15	23·5	32	46	63	75·3	87·7	100
Ships with forecastle and detached bridge	II	0	6·3	12·7	19	27·5	36	46	63	75·3	87·7	100

Percentages at intermediate lengths of superstructures shall be obtained by linear interpolation.

(3) For ships of type 'B'
(a) Where the effective length of a bridge is less than 0·2 L, the percentages shall be obtained by linear interpolation between lines I and II.
(b) Where the effective length of a forecastle is more than 0·4 L, the percentages shall be obtained from line II.
(c) Where the effective length of a forecastle is less than 0·07 L, the above percentages shall be reduced by:

$$5 \times \frac{(0\cdot07\ L - f)}{0\cdot07\ L}$$

where f is the effective length of the forecastle.

REGULATION 38

SHEER

General
(1) The sheer shall be measured from the deck at side to a line of reference drawn parallel to the keel through the sheer line at amidships.
(2) In ships designed with a rake of keel, the sheer shall be measured in relation to a reference line drawn parallel to the design load waterline.
(3) In flush deck ships and in ships with detached superstructures the sheer shall be measured at the freeboard deck.
(4) In ships with topsides of unusual form in which there is a step or break in the topsides, the sheer shall be considered in relation to the equivalent depth amidships.
(5) In ships with a superstructure of standard height which extends over the whole length of the freeboard deck, the sheer shall be measured at the superstructure deck. Where the height exceeds the standard the least difference (Z) between the actual and standard heights shall be added to each end ordinate.

Similarly, the intermediate ordinates at distances of $\frac{1}{6}$ L and $\frac{1}{3}$ L from each perpendicular shall be increased by 0·444 Z and 0·111 Z respectively.
(6) Where the deck of an enclosed superstructure has at least the same sheer as the exposed freeboard deck, the sheer of the enclosed portion of the freeboard deck shall not be taken into account.
(7) Where an enclosed poop or forecastle is of standard height with greater sheer than part of the freeboard deck, or is of more than standard height, an addition to the sheer of the freeboard deck shall be made as provided in paragraph (12) of this Regulation.

Standard Sheer Profile
(8) The ordinates of the standard sheer profile are given in the following table.

STANDARD SHEER PROFILE
(where L is in ft)

Station		Ordinate (in in)		Factor
	After Perpendicular	0·1	L +10	1
After	⅙ L from AP	0·0444	L +4·44	3
half	⅓ L from AP	0·0111	L +1·11	3
	Amidships		0	1
	Amidships		0	1
Forward	⅓ L from FP	0·0222	L +2·22	3
half	⅙ L from FP	0·0888	L +8·88	3
	Forward Perpendicular	0·2	L +20	1

Measurement of variation from standard sheer profile

(9) Where the sheer profile differs from the standard, the four ordinates of each profile in the forward or after half shall be multiplied by the appropriate factors given in the table of ordinates. The difference between the sums of the respective products and those of the standard divided by 8 measures the deficiency or excess of sheer in the forward or after half. The arithmetical mean of the excess or deficiency in the forward and after halves measures the excess or deficiency of sheer.

(10) Where the after half of the sheer profile is greater than the standard and the forward half is less than the standard, no credit shall be allowed for the part in excess and deficiency only shall be measured.

(11) Where the forward half of the sheer profile exceeds the standard, and the after portion of the sheer profile is not less than 75 per cent of the standard, credit shall be allowed for the part in excess; where the after part is less than 50 per cent of the standard no credit shall be given for the excess sheer forward. Where the after sheer is between 50 per cent and 75 per cent of the standard, intermediate allowances may be granted for excess sheer forward.

(12) Where sheer credit is given for a poop or forecastle the following formula shall be used:

$$s = \frac{y}{3} \frac{L^I}{L}$$

Where s = sheer credit, to be deducted from the deficiency or added to the excess of sheer.

    y = difference between actual and standard height of super-structure at the end of sheer.

L′=mean enclosed length of poop or forecastle up to a maximum length of 0·5 L.

L=length of ship as defined in Regulation 3(1) of this Annex.

The above formula provides a curve in the form of a parabola tangent to the actual sheer curve at the freeboard deck and intersecting the end ordinate at a point below the superstructure deck a distance equal to the standard height of a superstructure. The superstructure deck shall not be less than standard height above this curve at any point. This curve shall be used in determining the sheer profile for forward and after halves of the ship.

Correction for variations from standard sheer profile

(13) The correction for sheer shall be the deficiency or excess of sheer (see paragraphs (9) to (11) inclusive of this Regulation), multiplied by

$$0.75 - \frac{S}{2L}$$

where S is the total length of enclosed superstructures.

Addition for deficiency in sheer

(14) Where the sheer is less than the standard, the correction for deficiency in sheer (see paragraph (13) of this Regulation) shall be added to the freeboard.

Deduction for excess sheer

(15) In ships where an enclosed superstructure covers 0·1 L before and 0·1 L abaft amidships, the correction for excess of sheer as calculated under the provisions of paragraph (13) of this Regulation shall be deducted from the freeboard; in ships where no enclosed superstructure covers amidships, no deduction shall be made from the freeboard; where an enclosed superstructure covers less than 0·1 L before and 0·1 L abaft amidships, the deduction shall be obtained by linear interpolation. The maximum deduction for excess sheer shall be at the rate of 1½ in per 100 ft of length.

REGULATION 39

MINIMUM BOW HEIGHT

(1) The bow height defined as the vertical distance at the forward perpendicular between the waterline corresponding to the assigned

summer freeboard and the designed trim and the top of the exposed deck at side shall not be less than:

for ships below 820 ft in length,

$$0.672 \text{ L} \left(1 - \frac{\text{L}}{1640}\right) \frac{1.36}{C_b + 0.68} \text{ in;}$$

for ships of 820 ft and above in length,

$$275.6 \frac{1.36}{C_b + 0.68} \text{ in;}$$

where L is the length of the ship in ft,

C_b is the block coefficient which is to be taken as not less than 0.68.

(2) Where the bow height required in paragraph (1) of this Regulation is obtained by sheer, the sheer shall extend for at least 15 per cent of the length of the ship measured from the forward perpendicular. Where it is obtained by fitting a superstructure, such superstructure shall extend from the stem to a point at least 0.07 L abaft the forward perpendicular, and it shall comply with the following requirements:

(a) for ships not over 328 ft in length it shall be enclosed as defined in Regulation 3(10), and

(b) for ships over 328 ft in length it need not comply with Regulation 3(10) but shall be fitted with closing appliances to the satisfaction of the Administration.

(3) Ships which, to suit exceptional operational requirements, cannot meet the requirements of paragraphs (1) and (2) of this Regulation may be given special consideration by the Administration.

REGULATION 40

MINIMUM FREEBOARDS

Summer Freeboard

(1) The minimum freeboard in summer is the freeboard derived from the Tables in Regulation 28 as modified by the corrections in Regulation 27, as applicable, 29, 30, 31, 32, 37, 38 and, if applicable, 39.

(2) The freeboard in salt water, as calculated in accordance with paragraph (1) of this Regulation, but without the correction for deck line, as provided by Regulation 32, shall not be less than 2 in. For ships having in position 1 hatchways with covers which do not comply with the requirements of Regulations 15(7), 16 or 26—pontoon covers—the freeboard shall not be less than 6 in.

Tropical Freeboard

(3) The minimum freeboard in the Tropical Zone shall be the freeboard obtained by a deduction from the summer freeboard of one forty-eighth of the summer draught measured from the top of the keel to the centre of the ring of the load line mark.

(4) The freeboard in salt water, as calculated in accordance with paragraph (1) of this Regulation, but without the correction for deck line, as provided by Regulation 34, shall not be less than 2 in. For ships in position 1 hatchway with covers which do not comply with the requirements of Regulations 15(7), 16 or 26—pontoon covers—the freeboard shall be not less than 6 in.

Winter Freeboard

(5) The minimum freeboard in winter shall be the freeboard obtained by an addition to the summer freeboard of one forty-eighth of summer draught, measured from the top of the keel to the centre of the ring of the load line mark.

Winter North Atlantic Freeboard

(6) The minimum freeboard for ships of not more than 328 ft in length which enter any part of the North Atlantic defined in the Regulations, during the winter seasonal period shall be the winter freeboard plus 2 in. For other ships, the Winter North Atlantic Freeboard shall be the winter freeboard.

Fresh-water Freeboard

(7) The minimum freeboard in fresh water of unit density shall be obtained by deducting from the minimum freeboard in salt water:

$$\frac{\triangle}{40\ T}\ \text{in.}$$

where $\triangle$ = displacement in salt water in tons at the summer load waterline

T = tons per in immersion in salt water at the summer load waterline.

(8) Where the displacement at the summer load waterline cannot be certified, the deduction shall be one forty-eighth of summer draught, measured from the top of the keel to the centre of the ring of the load line mark.

REGULATION 41

SPECIAL REQUIREMENTS FOR SHIPS ASSIGNED TIMBER FREEBOARDS

Regulations 41 to 44 inclusive apply only to ships to which timber load lines are assigned.

REGULATION 42

DEFINITIONS

(1) *Timber deck cargo.* The term 'timber deck cargo' means a cargo of timber carried on an uncovered part of a freeboard or superstructure deck. The term does not include wood pulp or similar cargo.

(2) *Timber load line.* A timber deck cargo may be regarded as giving a ship a certain additional buoyancy and a greater degree of protection against the sea. For that reason, ships carrying a timber deck cargo may be granted a reduction of freeboard calculated according to the provisions of Regulation 45 and marked on the ship's side in accordance with the Regulations. However, in order that such special freeboard may be granted and used, the timber deck cargo shall comply with certain conditions which are laid down in Regulation 44, and the ship itself shall also comply with certain conditions relating to its construction which are set out in Regulation 43.

REGULATION 43

CONSTRUCTION OF SHIP

Superstructure
(1) Ships shall have a forecastle of at least standard height and a length of at least 0·07 L. In addition, if the ship is less than 328 ft in length, a poop of at least standard height, or a raised quarter-deck with either a deckhouse or a strong steel hood of at least the same total height shall be fitted aft.

Double-bottom tanks
(2) Double-bottom tanks where fitted within the midship half length of the ship shall have adequate watertight longitudinal subdivision.

Bulwarks

(3) The ship shall be fitted either with permanent bulwarks at least 39½ in in height, specially stiffened on the upper edge and supported by strong bulwark stays attached to the deck and provided with necessary freeing ports, or with efficient rails of the same height and of specially strong construction.

REGULATION 44

STOWAGE

General

(1) Openings in the weather-deck over which cargo is stowed shall be securely closed and battened down. The ventilators shall be efficiently protected.

(2) Timber deck cargo shall extend over at least the entire available length which is the total length of the well or wells between superstructures. Where there is no limiting superstructures at the after end, the timber shall extend at least to the after end of the aftermost hatchway. The timber shall be stowed as solidly as possible to at least the standard height of the superstructure.

(3) On a ship within a seasonal winter zone in winter, the height of the deck cargo above the weather-deck shall not exceed one-third of the extreme breadth of the ship.

(4) The timber deck cargo shall be compactly stowed, lashed and secured. It shall not interfere in any way with the navigation and necessary work of the ship.

Uprights

(5) Uprights, when required by the nature of the timber, shall be of adequate strength considering the breadth of the ship; the spacing shall be suitable for the length and character of timber carried, but shall not exceed 9·8 ft. Strong angles or metal sockets or equally efficient means shall be provided for securing the uprights.

Lashings

(6) Timber deck cargo shall be efficiently secured throughout its length by independent overall lashings spaced not more than 9·8 ft apart. Eye plates for these lashings shall be efficiently attached to the sheer strake or to the deck stringer plate at intervals of not more than 9·8 ft. The distance from an end bulkhead of a superstructure to the first eye plate shall be not more than 6·6 ft. Eye plates and lashings shall

be provided $23\frac{1}{2}$ in and 4·9 ft from the ends of timber deck cargoes where there is no bulkhead.

(7) Lashings shall be not less than $\frac{3}{4}$ in close link chain or flexible wire rope of equivalent strength, fitted with sliphooks and turnbuckles, which shall be accessible at all times. Wire rope lashings shall have a short length of long link chain to permit the length of lashings to be regulated.

(8) When timber is in lengths less than 11·8 ft the spacing of the lashings shall be reduced or other suitable provisions made to suit the length of timber.

(9) All fittings required for securing the lashings shall be of strength corresponding to the strength of the lashings.

Stability

(10) Provision shall be made for a safe margin of stability at all stages of the voyage, regard being given to additions of weight, such as those due to absorption of water and icing and to losses of weight such as those due to consumption of fuel and stores.

Protection of crew, access to machinery spaces, etc.

(11) In addition to the requirements of Regulation 25(5) guard rails or life lines spaced not more than 13 in apart vertically shall be provided on each side of the deck cargo to a height of at least 39 in above the cargo.

Steering arrangements

(12) Steering arrangements shall be effectively protected from damage by cargo and, as far as practicable, shall be accessible. Efficient provision shall be made for steering in the event of a breakdown in the main steering arrangements.

REGULATION 45

COMPUTATION FOR FREEBOARD

(1) The minimum summer freeboards are computed in accordance with Regulations 27(5), 27(6), 28, 29, 30, 31, 32, 37 and 38, except that Regulation 37 is modified by substituting the following percentages for those given in Regulation 37:

Total effective Length of Superstructures

	0	0·1 L	0·2 L	0·3 L	0·4 L	0·5 L	0·6 L	0·7 L	0·8 L	0·9 L	1·0 L
Percentage of deduction for all types of super-structure	20	31	42	53	64	70	76	82	88	94	100

Percentages at intermediate lengths of superstructures shall be obtained by linear interpolation.

(2) The Winter Timber Freeboard shall be obtained by adding to the Summer Timber Freeboard one thirty-sixth of the moulded summer timber draught.

(3) The Winter North Atlantic Timber Freeboard shall be the same as the Winter North Atlantic Freeboard prescribed in Regulation 40(6).

(4) The Tropical Timber Freeboard shall be obtained by deducting from the Summer Timber Freeboard one forty-eighth of the moulded summer timber draught.

(5) The Fresh Water Timber Freeboard shall be computed in accordance with Regulation 40(7) based on the summer timber load waterline.

Deck-line and load-line mark

The deck-line and load-line marks which are placed on both sides of the ship amidships are illustrated in Figures 71 and 72. The horizontal deck line, 12 in in length and 1 in in breadth, has its upper edge passing through the point where the continuation outwards of the upper surface of the freeboard deck intersects the outer surface of the shell as shown in Figure 71.

The load-line mark consists of a ring 12 in outside diameter and 1 in wide which is intersected by a horizontal line 18 in in length and 1 in in breadth, the upper edge of which passes through the centre of the ring. The centre of the ring is at amidships and at a distance equal to the assigned summer freeboard measured vertically below the upper edge of the deck line as shown in Figure 72. The lines indicating the load line assigned in accordance with the regulations are horizontal 9 in in length and 1 in in breadth at right-angles to a vertical line 1 in in breadth marked at a distance of 21 in forward of the centre of the ring as shown in Figure 72.

Q

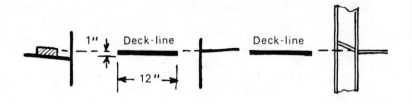

71 Deck-line mark

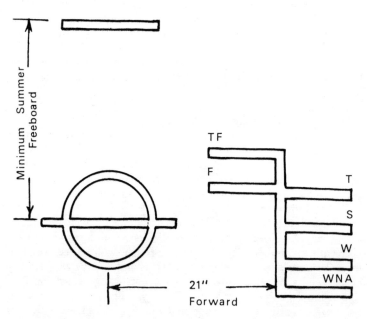

72 Load-line marks

The meaning of the letters on the various load-line marks are as follows:

Letters of Assigning Authority—size 4½ in in height and 3 in in width—LR=Lloyd's Register; AB=American Bureau; GL=Germanischer Lloyd; BV=Bureau Veritas; NV=Norske Veritas; NK= Nippon Kaiji Kyokai.

Load Lines:

S=Summer	T=Tropical
W=Winter	F=Fresh Water

WNA= Winter North Atlantic. TF=Tropical Fresh Water

These load lines are placed forward of the centre of the ring with TF and F abaft the vertical line (Figure 72).

Where timber freeboards are assigned the timber load lines are marked in addition to the ordinary load lines.

L=timber load line precedes the markings given above such as LS, LW, etc. (Figure 73).

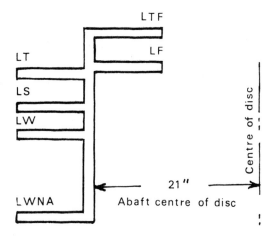

73 Timber load-line marks

The timber markings are placed abaft the centre of the ring.

The ring, lines and letters are painted in white or yellow on a dark ground or in black on a light ground. They are also permanently marked on the sides of the ships to the satisfaction of the Administration.

FREEBOARD CALCULATION—1966 REGULATIONS

A vessel has been selected the arrangement of which will cover the major cases that normally arise. The draught has been calculated as a Type A and as a Type B vessel.

The principal particulars are as follows:

Freeboard length (L) = 500 ft. 0 in. to centreline of rudder stock

Breadth moulded (B) = 68 ft. 0 in. Depth moulded = 39 ft. 3 in.

Thickness of stringer = 1 in. Thickness of keel = 7/8 in.

No deck sheathing.

Moulded displacement at moulded draught 85 per cent of least moulded depth = 23830 tons.

Length of forecastle 52 ft. Height 10 ft.

Length of bridge 36 ft. Curved 4·5 ft. Height 8 ft. Width (b) 64 ft.

Length of poop 108 ft. Curved 4·5 ft. Height 8 ft.

Sheer ordinates at intervals of one-sixth of L from the after terminal: 16, 2·25, 0, 0, 0, 5·44, 18 in.

Forecastle height at F.P. = 13·6 ft. Poop height at A.P. = 8·8 ft.

The calculation is presented in tabular form as Table 7 and subsidiary items are indicated below.

$$\text{Table depth} = \frac{L}{15} = \frac{500}{15} = 33\cdot33 \text{ ft.}$$

$$\text{Block Coefficient} = \frac{V}{LBd} = \frac{23830 \times 35}{500 \times 68 \times 39\cdot25 \times 0\cdot85} = 0\cdot736$$

Forecastle: mean covered length (S) = 52 ft.; (0·07L = 35 ft.; 0·4L = 200 ft.)

Bridge: mean covered length (S) = 36 + $\frac{2}{3}$ × 4·5 = 39 ft.

$$\text{effective length (E)} = 39 \times \frac{64}{68} = 36\cdot71 \text{ ft.}; (0\cdot2L = 100 \text{ ft.})$$

Poop: mean covered length (S) = 108 + $\frac{2}{3}$ × 4·5 = 111 ft.

TABLE 7

SHIP'S NAME   BUILDER'S NO.   DATE

Length on waterline (LW) at 85% of least moulded depth $\left\{ \begin{array}{l} \text{LW} \times 0.96 = 516 \times 0.96 = 495.4 \text{ ft.} \\ \text{to CL of rudder stock} = 500 \text{ ft.} \end{array} \right.$

Type:

Freeboard length (L) = 500 ft.   Breadth mld. = 68 ft.   Depth mld. amidships = 39 ft. 3 in.
Displ. mld. at 85% depth mld. = 23890 tons; C_b = 0.736. Least mld. depth = 39 ft. 3 in.

DEPTH FOR FREEBOARD (D)

			DEPTH CORRECTION
Depth mld.	=	39′ 3″	(a) Where D is greater than table depth (L/15)
Stringer plate	=	1″	(D−L/15) R = (39.33−33.33) 3 = 18 in.
Sheathing on exposed deck			(b) Where D is less than L/15 (if allowed)
$T\left(\dfrac{L-S}{L}\right)$	=		(L/15−D) R =
			(c) If restricted by super^E
Depth for Freeboard (D)		39′ 4″	

DEDUCTION FOR SUPERSTRUCTURES

SUPER^E	MEAN COVERED LENGTH (ft.) (s)	HEIGHT (ft.)	HEIGHT CORRECTION	EFFECTIVE LENGTH (ft.) (E)
Forecastle	52	10		52
Bridge	39	8		36·71
Poop	111	8		111
R.Q.D.				
Trunk aft				
Do. for^D				
Total	202			199·71

Standard ht. of super^E and trunks = 7·5 ft.
Do.   R.Q.D. =
Deduction for complete super^E = 42 in.
Percentage covered S/L = 40·4 in.
     E/L = 39·94

% from table = 31
Deduction = 13·02 in.

TYPE 'B' SHIP

	LINE I	LINE II
% from table	23·5	27·5
Corrected for fo'cle less than 0·07L		
Interpolation for bridge less than 0·2L		24·97

Fo'c'le = 0·104L
Bridge = 0·734L

Deduction   10·49 in.

SHEER CORRECTION

Excess height of end superstructures
Poop or R.Q.D. at A.P. = 8·8-7·5 = 1·3 ft.
Forecastle at F.P. = 13·6-7·5 = 6·1 ft.

$$S = Y/3 \times \frac{L_1}{L}$$

$$\frac{1·3 \times 12}{3} \times \frac{111}{500} = 1·154 \quad Sa$$

$$\frac{6·1 \times 12}{3} \times \frac{52}{500} = 2·538 \quad Sf$$

Sum of standard sheer aft products = SA × 8/3 = 160
Do. for^D = SF × 8/3 = 320

Ratio $\dfrac{\text{Virtual sheer}}{\text{Standard sheer}}$ $\begin{cases} \text{Aft} \\ \text{For}^D \end{cases}$ = Deficient

Length of enclosed super^E $\begin{cases} \text{For}^D \text{ of } \otimes \\ \text{Aft do.} \end{cases}$ = not applicable

L

STATION	ACTUAL ORDINATE (ins.)	S.M.	PRODUCTS
A.P.	16	1	16
1/6L from A.P.	2·25	3	6·75
2/6L Do.	0	3	0
Amidships	0	1	0

Sum = 22·75
Add (16 × Sa) = 18·46
Sum of virtual sheer = 41·21
Allowable sum (a) = 41·21

STATION	ACTUAL ORDINATE (ins.)	S.M.	PRODUCTS
Amidships	0	1	0
2/6L from F.P.	0	3	0
1/6L Do.	5·44	3	16·32
F.P.	18	1	18

Sum = 34·32
Add (16 × Sf) = 40·61
Sum of virtual sheer = 74·93
Allowable sum (b) = 74·93
Do. = 74·93
(a) = 41·21
TOTAL = 116·14

Continued on next page

Continued

$$\text{Correction} = \frac{\text{Difference between sums of products}}{16} \left(0.75 - \frac{S}{2L} \right)$$

$$= \frac{160 + 320 - 116 \cdot 14}{16} \ (0.75 - 0.202) = 12 \cdot 46 \text{ in.}$$

If limited on account of midship superstructure:
If limited to maximum allowance of $1\frac{1}{2}$ in. per 100 ft. of length:

BOW HEIGHT
Minimum bow height:

For ships below 820 ft. length $= 0.672L \left(1 - \frac{L}{1640} \right) \frac{1.36}{C_b + 0.68} = 224 \text{ in.}$

For ships 820 ft. length and above $= 275 \cdot 6 \ \dfrac{1.36}{C_b + 0.68} = \qquad \text{in.}$

Actual bow height $=$ depth (D) $+$ sheer at F.P. $+$ fo'c'le ht., at F.P. $-$ draught mld. $= 23 \cdot 4$ ft. $= 280 \cdot 8$ in.

TABULAR FREEBOARD AND SUMMARY OF CORRECTIONS

	TYPE A			TYPE B		
TABULAR FREEBOARD (in.)		79				93·1
CORRECTION FOR SUPER-STRUCTURE LENGTH < 0.35 L						
CORRECTION FOR BLOCK COEFFICIENT	$\dfrac{0 \cdot 736 + 0 \cdot 68}{1 \cdot 36}$	82·25				96·93
OTHER CORRECTIONS	+	−		+	−	
DEPTH	18	—		18	—	
SUPERSTRUCTURE	—	13·02		—	10·49	
SHEER	12·46	—		12·46	—	
THICKNESS OF DECK AMIDSHIPS	—	—		—	—	
POSITION OF DECK LINE	—	—		—	—	
SCANTLINGS; FLOODA-BILITY	—	—		—	—	
BOW HEIGHT, ETC.	—	—		—	—	
	30·46	13·02	+ 17·44	30·46	10·49	+ 19·97

SUMMER FREEBOARD	=	99·69	= 116·90
SAY	⇌	8′ 3⅝″	9′ 8⅞″
DEPTH TO FREEBOARD DECK	=	39′ 4″	39′ 4″
SUMMER FREEBOARD	=	8′ 3⅝″	9′ 8⅞″
DRAUGHT MOULDED	=	31′ 0⅜″	29′ 7⅛″
KEEL THICKNESS	=	⅞″	⅞″
EXTREME DRAUGHT	=	31′ 1¼″	29′ 8″

APPENDIX II · GLOSSARY OF HULL TERMS

ABAFT Aft of; toward the stern from amidships.

ACCOMMODATION LADDER A portable ladder fastened to a platform attached to the side of the ship.

AFT Toward, at, or near the stern.

AFTER BODY That portion of the hull abaft amidships.

AFTER PEAK The compartment at the stern abaft the aftermost watertight bulkhead.

AIR-PIPE Fitted to water, water ballast and oil tanks and led to the upper deck to allow the escape of air when the tanks are being filled.

AMIDSHIPS The portion of the ship at half its length.

ANCHOR Used to hold a ship stationary when afloat, to which is attached the chain cable.

APERTURE The space between the rudder post and propeller post for the propeller.

ARDENCY The quality of a ship by which she tends to drive her head into the wind.

ARSE of a block. The lower portion of a wooden block.

ATHWARTSHIP Across the ship transversely, at right-angles to the fore and aft centre-line.

AWASH Level with the surface of the water.

AWNING A canvas protection over a ship's deck.

BACKSTAY A wire stay fitted aft from the mast as a support.

R

BALLAST Any solid or liquid weight placed in a ship to increase the draught, to change the trim or to regulate the stability.

BALLAST TANK A watertight compartment to hold water ballast.

BAR KEEL A solid keel of steel, rectangular in section, the lengths of which are scarphed together, and attached to the garboard strake of shell plating.

BARGE A flat-bottomed vessel for carrying cargo. When non-propelled is termed a 'dumb-barge'.

BATTEN To batten down is to secure the hatchway tarpaulin.

BEAM, PANTING Fitted in the fore part of the ship to prevent vibration.

BEAM KNEE The connection between the beam and the frame of a ship.

BEAMS The athwartship steel rolled sections supporting the deck plating.

BERTH Where a ship is tied up or docked; a place to sleep aboard; a bunk or bed.

BETWEEN DECKS The space between any two adjacent decks.

BEVEL The angle between the flanges of a frame or other member of the structure. When greater than a right-angle, open bevel; when less, closed.

BILGE Curved portion between the bottom and the side shell plating; drainage space within the ship.

BILGE KEEL An external fin fitted at the round of bilge to reduce rolling.

BILGE STRAKE Course of shell plating at the bilge.

BINNACLE A stand to accommodate the compass.

BITT Fitted for the purpose of securing ropes; also called a bollard.

BLUE-PETER A blue flag hoisted when the ship is ready to proceed on a voyage, rectangular in shape with a white square in the centre.

BOATSWAIN'S CHAIR A wooden seat in which a man may be hoisted, aloft, or lowered over the ship's side.

BOLLARD See bitt.

BOOBY-HATCH A covered entrance or companionway leading down to the tween decks.

BOOT-TOPPING A protective composition applied to the shell plating between the light and load waterlines.

BOW STOPPER Used to check the chain cable running outboard.

BREAK The end of a partial superstructure such as a poop, bridge or forecastle where it drops to the deck below.

BREAKER A wooden cask used for the carriage of fresh water.

BREAKWATER Fitted on the weather deck forward and so shaped as to cause the water shipped on the deck to run off quickly.

BREASTHOOK A triangular plate bracket joining port and starboard side stringers at the stem.

BREECHES BUOY A circular lifebuoy with a canvas breeches to permit a man sitting inside and being hauled along a rope from the ship to the shore.

BULKHEAD A transverse or longitudinal division of a ship.

BULWARK The plating fitted for protection at the sides of a ship on and above the weather deck.

BUNK A berth or bed.

BUTT The joint formed when two parts are placed edge to edge; the end joint between two plates.

BUTT STRAP A strap that overlaps the butt between two plates.

BUTTOCKS The fore and aft sections giving the longitudinal form of a ship used on the lines plan of a ship.

CABLE LENGTH An approximate measurement for length of chain cable, 600 ft, or almost one-tenth of a nautical mile.

CAISSON The watertight structure fitted to the entrance of a dry dock.

CAMBER The amount of curvature in a deck; also called round of beam.

CAPSTAN A revolving device with a vertical axis, used for heaving-in mooring lines.

CARGO BATTENS Strips of wood fitted inside the frames to keep cargo away from hull steelwork; also called sparring.

CARGO PORT Opening in ship's side for loading and unloading cargo.

CARLING A steel section fitted fore and aft between beams.

CAULKING The filling of the seams of wood planks with oakum; method of closing butts and seams of steel plating to make them watertight.

CEILING Wood covering placed over the tank top for its protection.

CHAIN LOCKER Where the cables are stowed at the fore end of a ship.

CHINE The intersection of the straight sides, or ends, with the flat bottom of a barge.

CLEAT A fitting having two horns around which ropes may be made fast; a clip on the frames to hold the cargo battens in place.

COAMING, HATCH The vertical plating bounding a hatchway.

COFFERDAM Narrow space between two bulkheads or floors that prevents leakage between adjoining compartments.

COMPANION The permanent covering to a ladderway.

COUNTER The overhanging portion of the stern.

COWL A hood-shaped top to a ventilator.

CRADLE The supporting structure to carry the ship on the sliding ways for launching.

CROW'S NEST Elevated look-out position near the top of the foremast.

DAVITS The supports under which the lifeboats are stowed and from which they are launched overboard.

DEAD FLAT The portion of a ship's structure that maintains the midship form.

DEADLIGHT A hinged or portable internal steel cover fitted to a side light.

DEADRISE Athwartship rise of bottom from keel to the bilge.

DEADWEIGHT The difference in displacement between the light and load waterlines.

DECK, FREEBOARD Deck to which the freeboard is measured.

DECLIVITY Inclination of ways on which ship slides during launching.

DEEP TANKS Tanks extending from top of double bottom up to or higher than the lowest deck. May be used for dry cargo, water ballast, or liquid cargo.

DEMURRAGE Charge made by shipowner or wharf owner for delay in unloading or loading.

DERRICK A wood spar or steel tube used for discharging or loading cargo.

DISPLACEMENT The weight of water displaced by the ship.

DISPLACEMENT. LIGHT The displacement of the ship complete and ready for sea but excluding cargo, fuel, fresh water and stores.

DISPLACEMENT. LOAD The displacement when the ship is floating at the maximum permissible draught.

DOG A clip for securing a door or hatch cover.

DOG SHORES The preventative shores fitted between sliding and ground ways. When these are released at the launch the ship is free to move.

DOLLY The steel bar used by the holder-up when a rivet is being clenched.

DOUBLE BOTTOM The space between the outer and inner bottoms used for water ballast, fresh water, oil fuel, etc.

DOUBLING A stiffening or second plate to provide additional strength.

DRAUGHT The depth of water at which the ship floats.

DRAUGHT MARKS Cut in on the stem and sternpost. The marks are at every 12 in, the figures being 6 in in depth.

DUNNAGE Battens fitted in the hold for the protection of the cargo.

DUTCHMAN A piece of wood or steel used to cover up a defective joint.

ENSIGN STAFF A flagstaff at the stern.

ENTRANCE The immersed body forward of the parallel body.

EQUIPMENT NUMBER A number used by Classification Societies to determine the size and number of anchors, cables and ropes for a ship.

EVEN KEEL When the draughts of the ship are the same forward and aft.

FAIR To smooth or fair up a ship's lines.

FAIRLEAD A fitting used to preserve or change the direction of a rope.

FALL The rope used with blocks.

FATHOM A unit of measurement, 6 linear ft, used in connection with depth of water and length of chain cable.

FAYING SURFACE The surface between two adjoining parts.

FENDERS Rubbing pieces fitted on the sides of the ship as a means of protection.

FIDLEY The top of the boiler casing.

FLARE The spreading out of the hull form from the vertical plane.

FLOODABLE LENGTH See Chapter IX.

FLOORS Transverse vertical plates in the double bottom.

FLOTSAM Portions of the ship's equipment that have gone overboard and are floating.

FLUSH DECK An upper deck without side to side erections.

FOREBODY That portion of the ship's body forward of the midship section.

FORECASTLE The superstructure on the upper deck at the fore end of a ship.

FOREFOOT The lower end of a vessel's stem which curves to meet the keel.

FORE PEAK The watertight compartment at the extreme forward end.

FREEBOARD The distance from the waterline to the upper surface of the freeboard deck at side.

FREEING PORT Openings in the bulwark plating for freeing deck of water.

FREIGHT Cargo.

GALLEY The ship's cookhouse.

GANGWAY A ladderway used for boarding a ship.

GARBOARD The strake of bottom shell plating adjacent to the keel plate.

GASKET Flexible material used for making doors or covers watertight.

GIG A light pulling boat.

GIMBALS The apparatus attached to the binnacle in which the compass is suspended.

GIRTING To measure the distance round the girth of a ship.

GOOSENECK A ventilator turned over at the head to prevent the entry of water.

GROMMET A soft ring used under a nut to maintain watertightness.

GROSS TONNAGE See Chapter VI.

GROUNDWAYS The fixed ways on which the sliding ways attached to the ship move when a ship is being launched.

GUDGEONS Bosses on the rudder post to take the rudder pintles, about which the rudder turns.

GUNWALE The junction of the upper deck with the shell plating.

GUNWALE BAR The angle bar at the gunwale.

GUSSET PLATE A bracket plate connecting side frames to inner bottom plating.

GYPSY A small drum attached to a winch or windlass.

HALYARDS Light lines used for hoisting flags or signals.

HATCHWAY Opening in a deck through which cargo is loaded or unloaded.

HAWSE PIPE Tube through which anchor chain is led.

HOGGING When a vessel drops at the extremities. The opposite is sagging.

HOLDS Spaces below deck for stowage of cargo.

HORNING The process of setting frames square to the keel.

HOUNDS The bands around the mast to take the shrouds.

HULK An empty vessel not capable of being self-propelled.

HYDROMETER An instrument used for obtaining the density of water.

INBOARD Inside the ship.

INNER BOTTOM Plating forming the top of the double bottom, also called tank top.

INTERCOSTAL A longitudinal girder, not continuous.

ISLAND A side to side erection but detached from other erections. The combination of a poop, bridge and forecastle is termed a three-island ship.

JACK STAFF A flagstaff at the bow.

JACOB'S LADDER A portable rope or wire ladder used over the ship's sides.

JETSOM Deck cargo thrown overboard for the safety of the ship.

JOGGLE To offset a plate so as to avoid the use of liners.

JOLLY BOAT A ship's boat.

JURY MAST A temporary mast.

KEEL BILGE External plate fitted at right-angles to shell plating at bilge to reduce rolling.

KING POST Vertical post fitted to support a derrick; also called samson post.

KNEE BEAM Bracket connecting beam and frame.

KNOT A unit of speed; one nautical mile (6080 ft) per hour.

KNUCKLE An abrupt change in direction of plating.

LAGGING Material used for insulation.

LANDING Longitudinal laps of plating.

LAP A joint in which one part overlaps the other.

LAYING OFF Developing the form of the ship on the mould loft floor.

LEE SIDE The opposite side of the ship to that which is exposed to the weather.

LEEWAY The amount a ship has deviated from the set course.

LIFEBUOY Circular shaped cork float.

LIFEJACKET A belt or jacket of cork or kapok.

LIGHT AND AIR SPACE See Chapter VI.

LIGHT WATERLINE The draught of the ship in the light condition.

LIGHTENING HOLE A hole cut in a structural member to reduce weight.

LIGHTER An open non-propelled barge

LIMBER HOLE A drain hole.

LINER A merchant ship engaged on a direct regular service.

LINES The plans that show the form of the ship.

LIST Inclination of ship from the upright.

LOAD WATERLINE This corresponds to the ship's maximum draught.

LOG BOOK The official book containing the records of the voyage inserted by the master of the ship.

LONGITUDINALS For and aft structural members.

LOUVRE A small ventilatior.

MANHOLE A hole in tank top, etc., to provide access.

MARGIN LINE An imaginary line drawn 3 in below and parallel to the bulkhead deck. See Chapter IX.

MARGIN PLATE The outer boundary of the double bottom.

MESSROOM Dining room for officers or crew.

METACENTRE See Chapter V.

METACENTRIC HEIGHT See Chapter V.

MIDSHIPS Middle of the ship's length.

MOORING RING Oval casting set in the bulwark plating through which the mooring lines are passed.

MOULDED LINE The outside edge of the frame and is the line which appears on the 'lines' plan.

MOULDS Battens made in the mould loft for transferring information.

NAUTICAL MILE Equal to 6080 ft.

NEAP TIDE When the difference between the rise and fall of the tides is very small; the opposite to which is the spring tide.

NEUTRAL AXIS See Chapter II.

OAKUM Hemp fibre used for caulking seams of planks.

OFFSETS Term used for co-ordinates of a ship's shape or form.

ORLOP The lowest deck.

OUTBOARD Towards the ship's side; outside the hull.

OVERHANG The amount of the stern projecting beyond the after perpendicular.

OXTER PLATE A steel plate that fits around the upper part of the rudder post.

PACKET A passenger ship.

PADDLE BOX Covering over the paddles.

PAINTER A rope in a lifeboat ready for use in towing or making fast.

PANTING The pulsating in and out of the bow shell plates as the ship rises and plunges in the sea.

PARALLEL MIDDLE BODY The portion of the immersed body which retains the same area and shape as the midship section.

PEAK TANKS The compartments at the extreme ends of the ship which are normally used as ballast tanks.

PERMEABILITY The percentage of a space in the ship which could be occupied with water.

PILLARS Supports to the decks.

PINNACE A small motor boat.

PINTLES The pins that hinge the rudder to the gudgeons on the rudder post.

PITCH The distance a propeller will advance in one revolution.

PITCHING The action of a ship in moving to the crest and descending into the trough of a wave.

PITTING The corroding action on steel plates makes surface indentations.

PLIMSOLL MARKS The freeboard marks on the ship's sides.

PLUMBER BLOCKS The supports to the propeller shaft fitted in the tunnel.

POOP The after superstructure on the upper deck.

POPPETS The built-up vertical supports to the ends of the ship on the launching ways.

PORTHOLE A hinged circular glass window in the ship's side or deckhouse.

PORT SIDE The left side of a ship when looking forward.

PREVENTER An additional stay to support the mast.

PROPELLER A revolving screw-like device that drives the ship through the water.

QUADRANT The fitting attached to the rudder head and connected to the steering gear.

QUARTERS Living or sleeping rooms.

RABBET The portion cut out to receive the ends or butts of planks.

RACKING The tendency of the structure to alter form.

RAIL The wood member on top of the bulwark.

RAKE The inclination from the vertical of the masts, funnel, etc.

REAMING The process of making a rivet hole larger.

RIBBANDS Battens holding the frames in position ready for plating.

RUDDER A device used to steer a vessel.

RUDDER POST The aft post of the sternframe to which the rudder is attached.

RUN The immersed body aft of the parallel body.

SAGGING When a vessel drops at the middle of length. The opposite to hogging.

SCANTLINGS The thickness of plating, etc.

SCUPPERS Drains from decks to carry off rain or sea water.

SCUTTLES Side lights or portholes.

SETTLING TANK Oil-fuel tank used for separating entrained water from the oil.

SHEATHING The wood planks covering a deck.

SHEER The longitudinal curvature of the deck at side between the ends of the ship.

SHEER PLAN A plan showing the profile of the ship.

SHEER STRAKE The strake of shell plating at deck level.

SHELL EXPANSION A plan showing the disposition and thickness of all plates comprising the shell plating.

SHELL PLATING The plates forming the outer side of the hull.

SHIFTING BOARDS Portable wood planking fitted fore and aft in holds to prevent the shift of grain or similar cargo.

SHORE A prop used for support on the building berth or in dry dock.

SILL The height of an opening above the deck.

SKYLIGHT A framework over accommodation or engine with glass inserted to admit light and air to the space below.

SLIP The building berth.

SOUNDING PIPE A pipe led from the upper deck to the bottom of a tank or double bottom and used to ascertain the depth of water or liquid therein.

SPECTACLE FRAME The casting which projects from the ship's sides to take the bearings of the propeller shafts of a twin screw ship.

STABILITY See Chapter V.

STANCHION Vertical column supporting decks or girders; also called a pillar.

STANDING RIGGING Fixed rigging supporting the masts.

STARBOARD The right-hand side of a ship when looking forward; opposite to port.

STEERING GEAR The gear which turns the rudder.

STEM The casting at the extreme fore end of a ship.

STERN The aftermost end of a ship.

STERNPOST The casting at the aft end of a ship in way of the propeller.

STERN TUBE The bearing which supports the propeller shaft where it emerges from the ship.

STOW To put away; to stow cargo in a hold.

STRAKE A continuous course or row of plates on deck or shell.

STRINGER The strake of deck plating at the ship's side.

STRUM A strainer fitted to the end of a suction pipe.

TAIL SHAFT The aftermost length of shaft to which the propeller is attached.

TARPAULIN Waterproof canvas cover secured over non-watertight hatch covers.

TELEGRAPH An apparatus to transmit orders from the ship's bridge to the engine room.

TELEMOTOR A device to operate the control valves of the steering engine.

TEMPLATE A mould or pattern.

THRUST RECESS A small compartment at the fore end of the tunnel at the engine room to accommodate the thrust block.

TIERS In rows.

TILLER The lever attached to the rudder.

TONNAGE See Chapter VI.

TOP HAMPER An undue amount of superstructure above the weather deck.

TOPSIDES The upper side of a ship above the water.

TRAMP A merchant ship not confined to definite ports, but sails to and from any port.

TRANSOM The aftermost transverse side frame.

TRANSVERSE At right-angles to the fore and aft centre-line.

TRAWLER A vessel engaged in fishing using a trawl along the sea bed.

TRIM The difference in draught forward and aft.

TUMBLE HOME The inclination inboard of the upper sides of a ship.

'TWEEN DECKS The space between two adjacent decks.

ULLAGE The quantity a tank or oil compartment lacks being full.

VEER To pay or ease out the chain cable.

WAKE The track left by a ship moving through the water.

WALL-SIDED A ship with perpendicular sides.

WARPS Ropes used to haul a ship into position.

WATER-LOGGED A vessel when full of water, but able to float.

WEIGH To take the weight of the anchor on the cable.

WELL The open deck space between erections.

WINCH A machine used for hoisting and lowering cargo.

WINDLASS The machine used for raising the anchor and chain cable.

YAW A ship which is not under proper control making the fore part move from side to side.

INDEX